East Germany: The History and Legacy of the Soviet Satellite State Established after World War II

By Charles River Editors

Edward Valachovic's picture of the Berlin Wall in 1975

About Charles River Editors

Charles River Editors is a boutique digital publishing company, specializing in bringing history back to life with educational and engaging books on a wide range of topics. Keep up to date with our new and free offerings with this 5 second sign up on our weekly mailing list, and visit Our Kindle Author Page to see other recently published Kindle titles.

We make these books for you and always want to know our readers' opinions, so we encourage you to leave reviews and look forward to publishing new and exciting titles each week.

Introduction

A picture of East German workers building the Berlin Wall

East Germany

"From Stettin in the Baltic to Trieste in the Adriatic an 'Iron Curtain' has descended across the continent. Behind that line lie all the capitals of the ancient states of Central Europe and Eastern Europe. Warsaw, Berlin, Prague, Vienna, Budapest, Belgrade, Bucharest and Sofia; all these famous cities and the populations around them lie in what I must call the Soviet sphere, and all are subject, in one form or another, not only to Soviet influence but to a very high and in some cases increasing measure of control from Moscow." – Winston Churchill, 1946

"Here in Berlin, one cannot help being aware that you are the hub around which turns the wheel of history. ... If ever there were a people who should be constantly sensitive to their destiny, the people of Berlin, East and West, should be they." - Martin Luther King, Jr.

In the wake of World War II, the European continent was devastated, and the conflict left the Soviet Union and the United States as uncontested superpowers. This ushered in over 45 years of the Cold War, and a political alignment of Western democracies against the Communist Soviet bloc that produced conflicts pitting allies on each sides fighting, even as the American and Soviet militaries never engaged each other.

Though it never got "hot," the Cold War was a tense era until the dissolution of the USSR, and nothing symbolized the split more than the Berlin Wall, which literally divided the city. Berlin had been a flashpoint even before World War II ended, and the city was occupied by the different Allies even as the close of the war turned them into adversaries. After the Soviets' blockade of West Berlin was prevented by the Berlin Airlift, the Eastern Bloc and the Western powers continued to control different sections of the city, and by the 1960s, East Germany was pushing for a solution to the problem of an enclave of freedom within its borders. West Berlin was a haven for highly-educated East Germans who wanted freedom and a better life in the West, and this "brain drain" was threatening the survival of the East German economy.

In order to stop this, access to the West through West Berlin had to be cut off, so in August 1961, Soviet premier Nikita Khrushchev authorized East German leader Walter Ulbricht to begin construction of what would become known as the Berlin Wall. The wall, begun on Sunday August 13, would eventually surround the city, in spite of global condemnation, and the Berlin Wall itself would become the symbol for Communist repression in the Eastern Bloc. It also ended Khrushchev's attempts to conclude a peace treaty among the Four Powers (the Soviets, the Americans, the United Kingdom, and France) and the two German states.

The wall would serve as a perfect photo-opportunity for two presidents (Kennedy and Reagan) to hammer the Soviet Communists and their repression, but the Berlin Wall would stand for nearly 30 years, isolating the East from the West. It is estimated about 200 people would die trying to cross the wall to defect to the West.

Things came to a head in 1989. With rapid change throughout Europe, the wall faced a challenge it could not contain, the challenge of democracy's spread. On the night of November 9, 1989, the Berlin Wall was effectively removed from the midst of the city it so long divided —removed with pick axes and sledgehammers, but also removed from the hearts and minds of the people on both sides who only hours before had thought the wall's existence insurmountable. As one writer put it, "No border guard, no wall, can forever shield repressive regimes from the power of subversive ideas, from the lure of freedom."

Of course, the Berlin Wall also literally divided West Germany from East Germany. Until the unification of the country again in 1990, East Germany was predicated on, fueled by, and in the end, contingent on, the superpowers' rivalry. The history of East Germany was a remarkable one, from its chaotic origins through its ossification as a Stalinist regime, until the country collapsed along with the Berlin Wall. And in many ways, the legacy of East Germany is still around today; not only is Germany still marked by the division, but in some respects, the old frontier still represents different expectations, social conditions, and worldviews.

East Germany: The History and Legacy of the Soviet Satellite State Established after World War II examines the controversial country and its place in the Cold War. Along with pictures and a bibliography, you will learn about East Germany like never before.

Germany at the End of World War II

The events that led to the construction of the Berlin Wall began 20 years earlier during World War II. As the Soviets turned the tide against the Nazi invasion of Russia, they were able to begin advancing west toward Germany themselves, but the Soviet armies would pay dearly for the advances they made on Germany after Hitler's invasion of Russia ended in failure: "According to the Soviet Union's estimates, the Red Army's losses in the war totaled more than 11 million troops, over 100,000 aircraft, more than 300,000 artillery pieces, and 100,000 tanks and self-propelled guns".[1] Such losses, coupled with the extreme suffering that the Soviet soldiers had experienced in the years before the attack on Berlin, ensured that the thirst for revenge would be high upon arrival. Moreover, as the Soviet armies moved through Eastern Europe, they were the first to discover concentration camps and death camps, furthering their anger. The comparison of Germany's standard of living with their own was another cause of outrage, all of which encouraged the men to show no mercy: "We will take revenge…revenge for all our sufferings…It's obvious from everything we see that Hitler robbed the whole of Europe to please his Fritzies…Their shops are piled high with goods from all the shops and factories of Europe.

---

[1] Evans, Richard. *The Third Reich at War.* 707.

We hate Germany and the Germans deeply. You can often see civilians lying dead in the street...But the Germans deserve the atrocities that they unleashed."[2]

Meanwhile, Germany's losses were mounting, and the Soviet armies were on the rebound, with an advantage of almost 5:1 over Germany in manpower, as well as superiority in tanks, aircraft, and artillery. Even with these major advantages, however, the race to Berlin would inflict a heavier toll on Soviet armies than they had yet seen, and with Berlin itself heavily defended by 30 mile deep defenses in multiple directions, the Soviets would eventually suffer over 100,000 lives just taking the city, along with 350,000 other casualties.

In the months leading up to the Battle of Berlin, there was a strange division amongst the German people regarding their fate. While Hitler called for the remainder of Berlin's population to take up arms and the most loyal responded to the call, many in Berlin were resigned to a seemingly inevitable defeat. In his study of Berlin in 1945, historian Antony Beevor described a city in which a grim humor had come to replace once hopeful and proud demeanors. Though humor was certainly an attempt at levity in the face of serious concerns, Germans nevertheless joked about the soon-to-arrive Russians, referring to LSR (Luftschutzraum air-raid shelters) as

---

[2] Ibid., 708.

actually standing for "Lernt scnhell Russich" ("Learn Russian quickly").[3] In the air raid shelters, Berliners regularly found themselves in crowded conditions, waiting out the bombing raids that were taking place on a regular basis in 1944. In a city of 3 million, Beevor explained how a tightly-packed and unsanitary atmosphere became an expected part of life in Berlin. By the year's end, much of the city's beauty and a great deal of its functionality had been destroyed.

---

[3] Beevor, Antony. *The Fall of Berlin 1945*. New York: Penguin Books, 2003.

A picture of damage done to Berlin during a 1944 air raid

Things weren't going any better for Germany to the west either. After the successful amphibious invasion on D-Day in June 1944, the Allies began racing east toward Germany and liberating France along the way. The Allies had landed along a 50 mile stretch of French coast, and despite suffering 8,000 casualties on D-Day, over 100,000 still began the march across the western portion of the continent. By the end of August 1944, the German army in France was shattered, with 200,000 killed or wounded and a further 200,000 captured. However, Hitler reacted to the news of invasion with glee, figuring it would give the Germans a chance to destroy the Allied armies that had water to their backs. As he put it, "The news couldn't be better. We have them where we can destroy them."

While that sounds delusional in retrospect, it was Hitler's belief that by splitting the Allied march across Europe in their drive toward Germany, he could cause the collapse of the enemy armies and cut off their supply lines. Part of Hitler's confidence came as a result of underestimating American resolve, but with the Soviets racing toward Berlin from the east, this final offensive would truly be the last gasp of the German war machine, and the month long campaign was fought over a large area of the Ardennes Forest, through France, Belgium and parts of Luxembourg. From an Allied point of view, the operations were commonly referred to as the Ardennes Offensive, while the German code phrase for the operation was Unternehmen Wacht am Rhein ("Operation Watch on the Rhine"), with the initial breakout going under the name of "Operation Mist." Today, it is best known as the Battle of the Bulge.

Regardless of the term for it, and despite how desperate the Germans were, the Battle of the Bulge was a massive attack against primarily American forces that inflicted an estimated 100,000 American casualties, the heaviest American loss in any battle of the war. However, while the German forces did succeed in bending and at some points even breaking through Allied lines (thus causing the "bulge" reflected in the moniker), the Germans ultimately failed. As Winston Churchill himself said of the battle, "This is undoubtedly the greatest American battle of the war, and will, I believe be regarded as an ever famous American victory."

The end of the Battle of the Bulge led to the historic Yalta Conference between Roosevelt, Churchill, and Stalin from January 30-February 3. It was not lost on anyone present that the Allies were pushing the Nazis back on both fronts and the war in Europe was ending. The Big Three held the conference with the intention of redrawing the post-war map, but within a few years, the Cold War divided the continent anyway. As a result, Yalta became a subject of intense controversy, and to some extent, it has remained controversial. Among the agreements, the Conference called for Germany's unconditional surrender, the split of Berlin, and German demilitarization and reparations. Stalin, Churchill and Roosevelt also discussed the status of Poland, and Russian involvement in the United Nations.

The three leaders at Yalta

By this time, Stalin had thoroughly established Soviet authority in most of Eastern Europe and made it clear that he had no intention of giving up lands his soldiers had fought and died for. The best he would offer Churchill and Roosevelt was the promise that he would allow free elections to be held, but at the same time, he made clear that the only acceptable outcome to any Polish election would be one that supported communism. One Allied negotiator would later describe Stalin's very formidable negotiating skills: "Marshal Stalin as a negotiator was the toughest proposition of all. Indeed, after something like thirty years' experience of international conferences of one kind and another, if I had to pick a team for going into a conference room, Stalin would be my first choice. Of course the man was ruthless and of course he knew his purpose. He never wasted a word. He never stormed, he was seldom even irritated."

The final question was over what to do with a conquered Germany. The British, Americans and Russians all wanted Berlin, and they knew that whoever held the most of it when the truce was signed would end up controlling the city. Thus, they spent the next several months pushing their generals further and further toward this goal. Since the Russians ultimately got there first, when the victorious Allies met in Potsdam in 1945, it remained Britain and America's task to convince Stalin to divide the country, and even the city of Berlin, between them. They ultimately accomplished this, but at a terrible cost: Russia acquired the previously liberated Austria.

With the race toward Berlin in full throttle, General Dwight D. Eisenhower's Allied armies were within 200 miles of the city, but his biggest battles now took place among his allies, as he now had to deal diplomatically with Churchill, Montgomery, and French war hero Charles de Gaulle. After crossing the Rhine River, General George Patton advised Eisenhower to make haste for Berlin, and British General Bernard Montgomery was confident that they could reach Berlin before the Soviets, but Eisenhower did not think it "worth the trouble".[4] Eisenhower's forces went on to capture 400,000 prisoners on April 1st in the Ruhr, but despite his success there, not everyone agreed with Eisenhower's decision, especially Winston Churchill. In Churchill's thinking, the decision to leave the taking of Berlin to the Soviets would leave lasting trouble on the European continent, a more pressing concern for the British than for Americans an ocean away. In tension-filled exchanges, Churchill made his position clear, but President Roosevelt was ill and had no stomach for angering the Soviets. For his part, Eisenhower saw his role as a purely military one, so he refused to "trespass" into political arenas that he was under the impression had been worked out at the Tehran and Yalta conferences. In fact, Roosevelt had promised Stalin that he could enter Berlin despite the obvious threat to postwar security for the European countries, and Eisenhower wanted to avoid being a pawn in the political maneuverings of the three leaders. As a result, his major concern was to avoid as many casualties as possible in the coming weeks of the war, and if the Russians were prepared to attack and had the better opportunity to do so, it would save lives of American soldiers who would otherwise have to fight their way in from the west.[5] Eisenhower did not share his

---

[4] World War II: A 50th Anniversary History. New York: Holt, 1989.288.

peers' (Patton and Montgomery, specifically) concerns of "arriving victorious in Berlin on top of a tank."[6]

Eventually, Eisenhower made the fateful choice not to move the American forces toward Berlin but to "hold a firm front on the Elbe" instead. In making this decision, Eisenhower left Berlin's capture to the Soviet army, and his decisions have been the cause of much debate ever since. The Allied armies in the west would thus concentrate on encircling the Ruhr Valley, the center of Germany's industry, instead of competing with the Soviets for control of the city.

[5] Humes, James C. Eisenhower and Churchill: The Partnership that Saved the World. Crown Publishing Group, 2010.
[6] Ibid.

Eisenhower

There were many concerns about the Soviet Union reaching Berlin, and all of them were understandable. Most people, especially the Germans, expected far worse treatment from Soviet conquerors than the British or Americans, especially since Hitler's attack on the Soviet Union (Operation Barbarossa) had been so unexpected that it stunned even Stalin into temporary inaction. Hitler and the Germans were going to pay dearly for the treatment that the Russians, both civilians and soldiers, had received at the hands of the German armies. Furthermore, the fear of a Soviet strategic advantage in Europe, anchored by a Soviet-controlled Berlin, loomed over both eastern and western European nations. Lastly, even if Stalin kept his word about the division of post-war Germany, allowing him unchallenged control was viewed as dangerous to a world with a weakened Britain and a United States looking to return to the isolation the Atlantic Ocean had previously provided.

Churchill and Roosevelt had always disagreed on Stalin's real motivations and limits, and Churchill needed to maintain strong ties to the Americans as the war came to a close. During one of the meetings between the three, Stalin suggested that once the German armies had been defeated, 50,000 soldiers should be executed by the conquering armies in vengeance for the losses Germany had inflicted on Europe. That suggestion horrified Churchill, who stormed out of the meeting, but Stalin followed to assure Churchill that all that had been said was in jest. Churchill had very little choice but to take Stalin at his word, but he was always far more cautious than Roosevelt when it came to trust in Stalin's judgment or word. In any case, he wrote a letter to Roosevelt after his exchange with Eisenhower in March in which he said, "I wish to place on record the complete confidence felt by

His Majesty's government in General Eisenhower and our pleasure that our armies are serving under his command and our admiration of his great and shining quality, character, and personality".[7] In a note he added to Eisenhower's copy of the letter, he expressed it would grieve him to know he had pained Eisenhower with his comments but still suggested that "we should shake hands with the Russians as far east as possible."[8]

By April 17, in a meeting between Eisenhower and Churchill, the fact that the Soviet army was positioned just over 30 miles from Berlin with overpowering men, artillery, and tanks convinced Churchill that the decision to allow the Soviets to lead the attack on the city was necessary. It is important to keep in perspective that Roosevelt's death just 5 days earlier likely played a role in Churchill's willingness to give in. Churchill had spent several years negotiating with both Stalin and Roosevelt, and he may have felt that time would not allow for further discussion on the matter. Eisenhower also was under pressure to end the war in Europe as soon as possible so that American forces and attention could be directed toward the fight against Japan. The campaign in Okinawa had just started and would last until June, and the extent of the carnage there made clear that Japan had no intention of surrendering anytime soon.

---

[7] Ibid.
[8] Ibid.

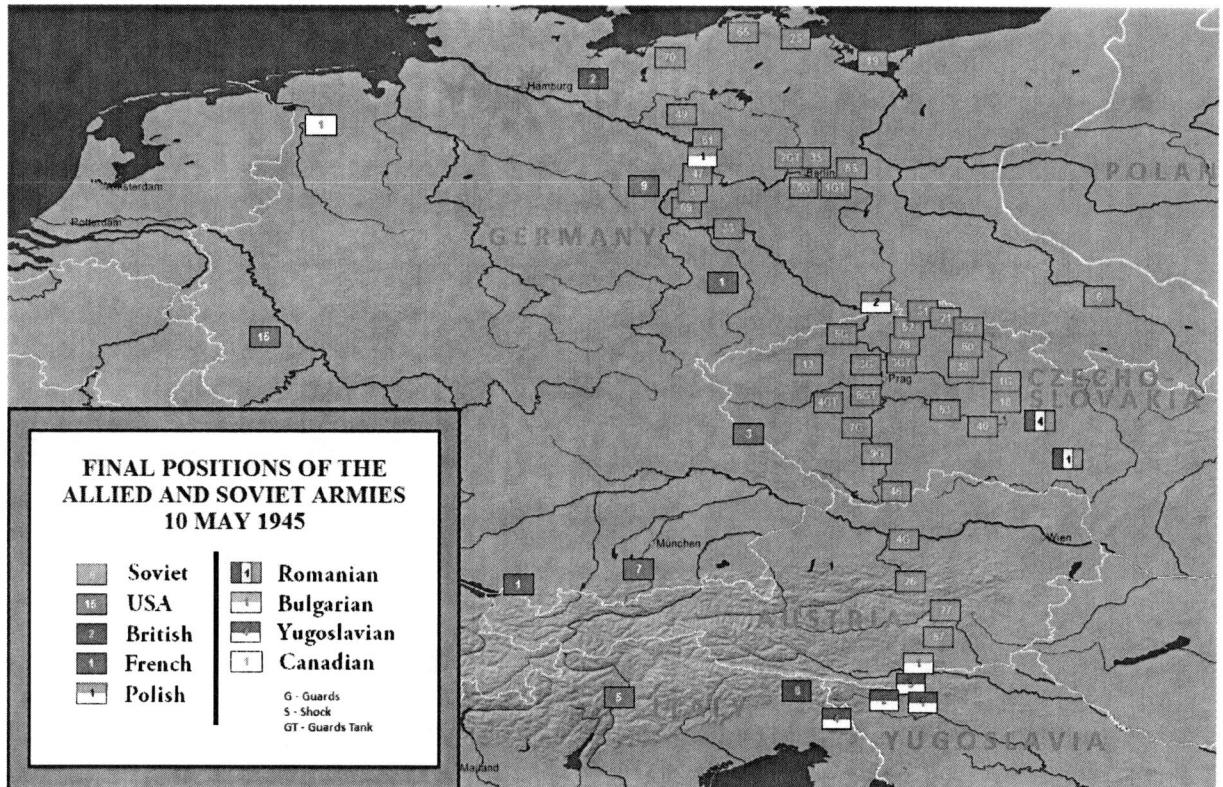

FINAL POSITIONS OF THE ALLIED AND SOVIET ARMIES 10 MAY 1945

Soviet		Romanian	
USA		Bulgarian	
British		Yugoslavian	
French		Canadian	
Polish			

G - Guards
S - Shock
GT - Guards Tank

The lines at the end of World War II

The Battle of Berlin ended with an inevitable Soviet triumph, but by the time Germany officially surrendered, the Soviets had suffered over 350,000 casualties and had lost thousands of artillery batteries and armored vehicles. The Germans had suffered upwards of 100,000 dead and over 200,000 wounded, not to mention the horrors visited upon the civilian population in the wake of the battle.

With the fighting mostly coming to an end on May 2, the chain of German surrenders in the field outside of Berlin took off like dominoes. Field Marshal Wilhelm Keitel signed Germany's unconditional surrender on May 7, and news of the final surrender of the Germans was celebrated as Victory in Europe (V-E) day on May 8, 1945. Churchill delivered the following remarks to cheering crowds:

"My dear friends, this is your hour. This is not victory of a party or of any class. It's a victory of the great British nation as a whole. We were the first, in this ancient island, to draw the sword against tyranny. After a while we were left all alone against the most tremendous military power that has been seen. We were all alone for a whole year.

There we stood, alone. Did anyone want to give in? Were we down-hearted? The lights went out and the bombs came down. But every man, woman and child in the country had no thought of quitting the struggle. London can take it. So we came back after long months from the jaws of death, out of the mouth of hell, while all the world wondered. When shall the reputation and faith of this generation of English men and women fail? I say that in the long years to come not only will the people of this island but of the world, wherever the bird of freedom chirps in human hearts, look back to what we've done and they will say 'do not despair, do not yield to violence and tyranny, march straightforward and die if need be-unconquered.'"

Bundesarchiv, Bild 183-R77799
Foto: o.Ang. | 8. Mai 1945

Pictures of the Germans' unconditional surrender on May 7

Of course, the announcement of surrender was met with a far different emotion among the Germans, as one Berliner remembered: "The next day, General Wilding, the commander of the German troops in Berlin, finally surrendered the entire city to the Soviet army. There was no radio or newspaper, so vans with loudspeakers drove through the streets ordering us to cease all resistance. Suddenly, the shooting and bombing stopped and the unreal silence meant that one ordeal was over for us and another was about to begin. Our nightmare had become a reality. The entire three hundred square miles of what was left of Berlin were now completely under control of the Red Army. The last days of savage house to house fighting and street battles had been a human slaughter, with no prisoners being taken on either side. These final days were hell. Our last remaining and exhausted troops, primarily children and old men, stumbled into imprisonment. We were a city in ruins; almost no house remained intact."

The controversy over Eisenhower's decision not to press for Berlin remains, but any debate over whether the Allied armies were in a position to take Berlin must acknowledge the fact that the most significant American forces were over 200 miles from Berlin in mid-April. Nonetheless, others point to smaller American forces that were within 50 miles of the city before being told to move in the opposite direction.

The strongest critiques of Eisenhower's decisions portray him as naïve about the consequences, or as an unwitting tool of the Soviets, but his defenders call his decision "dead on".[9] Soviet casualties in taking the city rivaled those lost by the Allies at the Battle of the Bulge, and considering the earlier agreements with Stalin,

---

[9] Kevin Baker, "General Discontent: Blaming Powell-And Eisenhower-For Not Having Pushed Through. (in the News)," American Heritage, November-December 2002, https://www.questia.com/read/1G1-93611493.

General Omar Bradley believed that the Americans would have to pay "a pretty stiff price to pay for a prestige objective, especially when we've got to fall back and let the other fellow take over."[10]

Eisenhower vigorously defended himself against criticism upon his return from the war, pointing out that those who criticized his position on the issue were not the ones who would have been forced to comfort the grieving mothers of soldiers killed in an unnecessary fight to take Berlin. During his 1952 presidential campaign, he faced further criticism, and in response, he emphasized his warnings about the danger of the Soviet threat to Europe rather than discuss his decision to stay away from Berlin. Historian Stephen Ambrose saw this attempt at self-salvation by Eisenhower as wishful thinking, and that there was no evidence of Eisenhower warning against the Soviet threat to Europe during his time as general: "The truth was that he may have wished by 1952 that he had taken a hard line with the Russians in 1945, but he had not".[11]

---

[10] Ibid.
[11] Ibid.

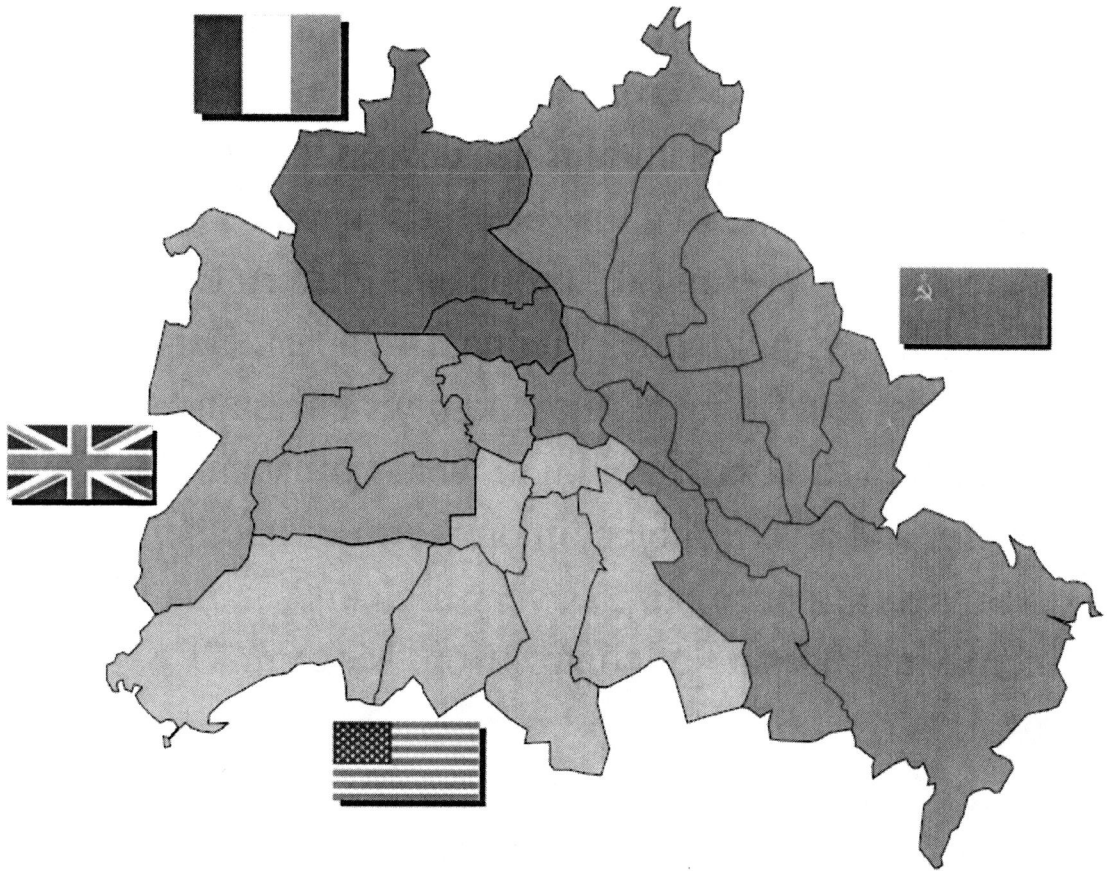

The different sections of Berlin at the end of the war

It was a famous moment commemorated as "East Meets West" when Soviet soldiers shook hands with other Allied soldiers in Germany near the end of the war, but nobody was under any illusions that they would continue to work well together after defeating their common enemy. In 1946, speaking to a war-weary world, Winston Churchill sounded what would become a famous warning about the aggression of the Soviet Union and the dangers of communism's spread while speaking to a group of college students at Westminster College in Fulton, Missouri: "I am sure you would wish me to state the facts as I see them to you, to place before you certain facts about the present position in Europe. From Stettin in the Baltic to Trieste in the Adriatic, an iron curtain has descended across the Continent. Behind that line lie all the capitals of the ancient states of Central Europe and Eastern Europe. Warsaw, Berlin, Prague, Vienna, Budapest, Belgrade, Bucharest and Sofia, all these famous cities and the populations around them lie in what I must call the Soviet sphere, and all are subject in one form or another, not only to Soviet influence but to a very high and, in many cases, increasing measure of control from Moscow."[12]

This "border" of states, the protection that Stalin claimed he needed to ensure his country's post-war security, included "Poland, Czechoslovakia, Hungary, Bulgaria, Romania, and the Soviet Occupation Zone in East Germany".[13] These areas would develop into Soviet satellite states, relying on the Soviet's for military defense, serving as the Soviet industrial plans' source for natural resources, and experiencing occasional crackdowns for showing signs of independence or unrest over the next 40 plus years.

At the same time, in the immediate aftermath of the war,

---

[12] Churchill, Winston. "The Sinews of Peace." Westminster College. Mississippi, Fulton. 5 Mar. 1946. *The Churchill Centre*. Web. 2 Feb. 2015.
[13] Rottman, 5.

the city of Berlin itself was divided into a French, British, American, and Soviet occupation zone. As on historian describes it, the division was uneven from the beginning: "[T]he victorious Allies unfurled a map and carved up the city - the houses then lining the south side of Bernauer Strasse wound up in the Soviet sector while the street itself and the sidewalk in front belonged to the French. By this cartographic fiat, some sectors of the population would find themselves economically rejuvenated by the Marshall Plan and reintroduced to bourgeois democratic society, while the rest were stuck with the Soviets.[14]

The city of Berlin was fully in Soviet hands between May and July of 1945, but they turned over the sectors they had agreed to back in 1944 to the British, Americans, and French. That said, in recognition of the last two months of the war, in which the Soviets had fought the Battle for Berlin at the cost of over 80,000 Soviet lives, the Soviets were given a much larger portion of the city than the rest of the Allies,[15] and as Germany divided into East and West along the borders of former German states, the city of Berlin ultimately fell well within East Germany's borders. In fact, Berlin was over 100 miles from the nearest point in what would become known as West Germany.

---

[14] Mark Ehrman, "Borders and Barriers," The Virginia Quarterly Review 83, no. 2 (2007), https://www.questia.com/read/1P3-1256577881.
[15] Ibid., 8.

General Georgy Zhukov, the Soviet hero of the war, established the communist party in Berlin,[16] and the decisions governing Soviet action became immediately political, despite their desire to be seen (by both sides) as purely motivated by military necessity. At first, the city was governed by an "Allied Control Council" of the four powers, with each country rotating control on a monthly basis. In *City on Leave: A History of Berlin 1945-1962*, Philip Windsor explains that the council was marked far more for argument and conflict than true governance. In fact, he argues, "All the Western Powers were…for different reasons, convinced that collaboration with the Soviet Union in Germany was their essential task. The struggle for the country came upon them almost unawares, and at the outset none was capable of answering the scarcely defined Russian threat. This threat would not become manifest until they were all forced to face the need of defining common economic policies and erecting a central German authority. But there was already one center in Germany where all were concerned together in a common assignation, and where the present government of the country was established. It offered a valuable, perhaps decisive, prize to Russia in the political conquest of the whole; and in the Rooseveltian terms which governed American policy, it provided the United States

---

[16] Philip Windsor, City on Leave: A History of Berlin, 1945-1962 (London: Chatto & Windus, 1963), 25, https://www.questia.com/read/11076907.

with the most practical test of Soviet intentions. *This was Berlin.*"[17]

Zhukov

In the early years of the Cold War, the West seemed to be in retreat as the Soviet Union succeeded in testing its own nuclear weapon, setting up puppet states in eastern Europe, and assisting the Chinese communists in winning a civil war over Western backed Chinese nationalist forces. Stalin subsequently hoped to continue to expand Russian influence by ordering a blockade of all supplies into West Berlin, hoping the West would cede the entire city to the Soviets. However, the United States and its allies were able to organize a massive airlift of supplies that kept the city of West Berlin supplied, and the Soviet Union and its German allies eventually stopped the blockade when they realized the West could continue to supply Berlin by air indefinitely. The Berlin Airlift was one of the first major confrontations of the Cold War, but it would hardly be the last; if anything, it was just the start for the contest over Berlin.

Picture of a plane participating in the Berlin Airlift in 1948

East Germany's Early Years

The ideological battle being played out in Berlin and greater Germany was fought between two spheres of influence led by the United States and the Soviet Union, but in the midst of the fight were the Germans, the people who had to live under the outcomes of policy, negotiations, and compromises formed by the push and pull of politics. Both sides of the conflict acknowledged that if the situation in Berlin ever required the use of nuclear weapons, the loss of German life would be devastating.

German leadership on both sides was required to maintain a delicate balance of working with the United States in the case of the West and the Soviets in the case of the East, as well as representing the interests and outcomes of their own people. For this reason, local leaders also played crucial roles in the division of Berlin and the construction of the wall.

Willy Brandt was the mayor of West Berlin from 1957-1966, and though he went on to serve as German chancellor and leader of a major German political party, it is for his time as mayor that he is best remembered. Brandt was a left-wing socialist who fled Germany during the Nazi reign, spending time in Scandinavia, but during the time of the Spanish Civil War, he came to distrust the Soviet Union and to champion the causes of German socialism rather than cooperation with the Soviet Union.

Brandt and Kennedy

As mayor of West Berlin, Brandt became the face for a group of over two million people whose lives hung in the balance of big decision-makers. President Kennedy invited Brandt to the White House in March 1961, and the English-speaking Brandt made a great impression on the young president. Kennedy hoped that he would be elected Chancellor of Germany in the next months, a desire that actually caused tension between Kennedy and the actual future chancellor.[18]

The future leader of communist East Germany began as a member of the Communist Party of Germany. Fleeing to Russia during the Nazi domination, Walter Ulbricht

[18] Kempe, Frederick. "West Berlin's Impertinent Mayor". *Reuters Blog: Analysis and Opinion.* 7 June 2011.

rose to power in Stalin's circles, supporting the purges and staying out of trouble. He returned to Germany as part of the Soviet occupation in 1945 and became the head of a new party, the Socialist Unity Party, which would control East Germany.[19] Ulbricht has been characterized by history as both a communist radical who pressured the Soviets into the construction of the wall, and as a leader more interested in independence and reforms that would move his country in a different direction than the other Soviet bloc nations.

Bundesarchiv, Bild 183-B0116-0010-038
Foto: Sturm, Horst | 16. Januar 1963

---

[19] Dennis Kavanagh, ed., A Dictionary of Political Biography (Oxford: Oxford University Press, 1998), 484, https://www.questia.com/read/34683386.

Ulbricht and Khrushchev

Konrad Adenauer was the first chancellor of Germany. Having been a prisoner of war under the Nazi regime, he was named the mayor of Berlin the day after the conclusion of the war, but the British dismissed him from this position. He formed the Christian Democratic Union party, which was anti-Socialist but concerned with the poor who had been devastated by Germany's economic hard times. Adenauer believed that friendliness with the United States, Britain, and France was necessary in order to protect Berlin and West Germany itself from the Soviets.[20]

---

[20] Dennis Kavanagh, ed., A Dictionary of Political Biography (Oxford: Oxford University Press, 1998), 4, https://www.questia.com/read/34683386.

Adenauer

With tensions between the West and East high, Germany
officially became two countries in 1949. West Germany
was founded on May 23, 1949, and four months later, on
October 7, the German Democratic Republic (DDR, from
the German: *Deutsche Demokratische Republik*) – East

Germany to non-Germans – officially came into existence. The Eastern half was closely linked to the Soviet government and rejected the existence of West Germany, claiming East Germany was "the only legal German state, to which the future of Germany belongs."[21]

Naturally, elections in the 1940s did not lead to a vibrant democracy, and when the Soviets handed control over to the SED government, the country was well on its way to Stalinization. An overbearing surveillance and state security apparatus denied basic freedoms to its citizens. The much-feared Stasi (State Security Service or *Staatssicherheitsdienst*) was formed in 1950. For his part, Ulbricht dreamed of building an East Germany that could compete with the West, instituting 5 year plans and insisting that "[t]he victory of the working people over the exploiters and slave holders is at the same time the victorious struggle for liberation by the German people".

Most historians agree that the German Democratic Republic was little more than a puppet state of the Soviet Union, especially during the early years of its existence. It is also true that the Federal Republic of Germany was not a sovereign nation until 10 years after the conclusion of the war. The Allies, led by the Americans, negotiated with West German authorities to reinstate the sovereignty of West Germany.

---

[21] Ibid. 11.

In the midst of this in 1952, Stalin came forward with a "peace note" offering to reorganize Germany and unite it as a neutral nation, but the West considered this nothing more than timely propaganda designed to cause division within West Germany about accepting the terms of the Allies for recognition of West Germany as an independent state. Stalin suggested not that the countries be united, but that West Germany gain her independence and not become a member of any western alliance. The Allies, as well as many West Germans, did not believe they could trust the Soviets to respect West Germany's neutrality and stated that the time for negotiation with Stalin had passed. American foreign policymakers such as Henry Kissinger also suggested that a neutral Germany would have to be very heavily armed in order to defend herself in the midst of Europe, especially with the Soviet satellite states all along her border. Since "a strong, unified Germany in the center of the continent pursuing purely national policy had proved incompatible with the peace of Europe[22]", this could not be an acceptable solution.

In 1952, the Inner German Border between East and West Germany was constructed by the East German government, and from then on, "the inner-German border became one of Cold War Europe's most menacing frontiers—an 858-mile death-strip of barbed wire fences,

[22] Wilke, Manfred. The Path to the Berlin Wall: Critical Stages in the History of Divided Germany. New York: Berghahn Books, 2014.88.

control points, watchtowers, mines, and, later, automatic shooting devices".[23] It is important to remember that while the rate of deaths for those attempting to cross the Berlin Wall between 1961 and 1989 is often estimated to be about 200, nearly another 700 East Germans were killed crossing the Inner German border during the same period.[24]

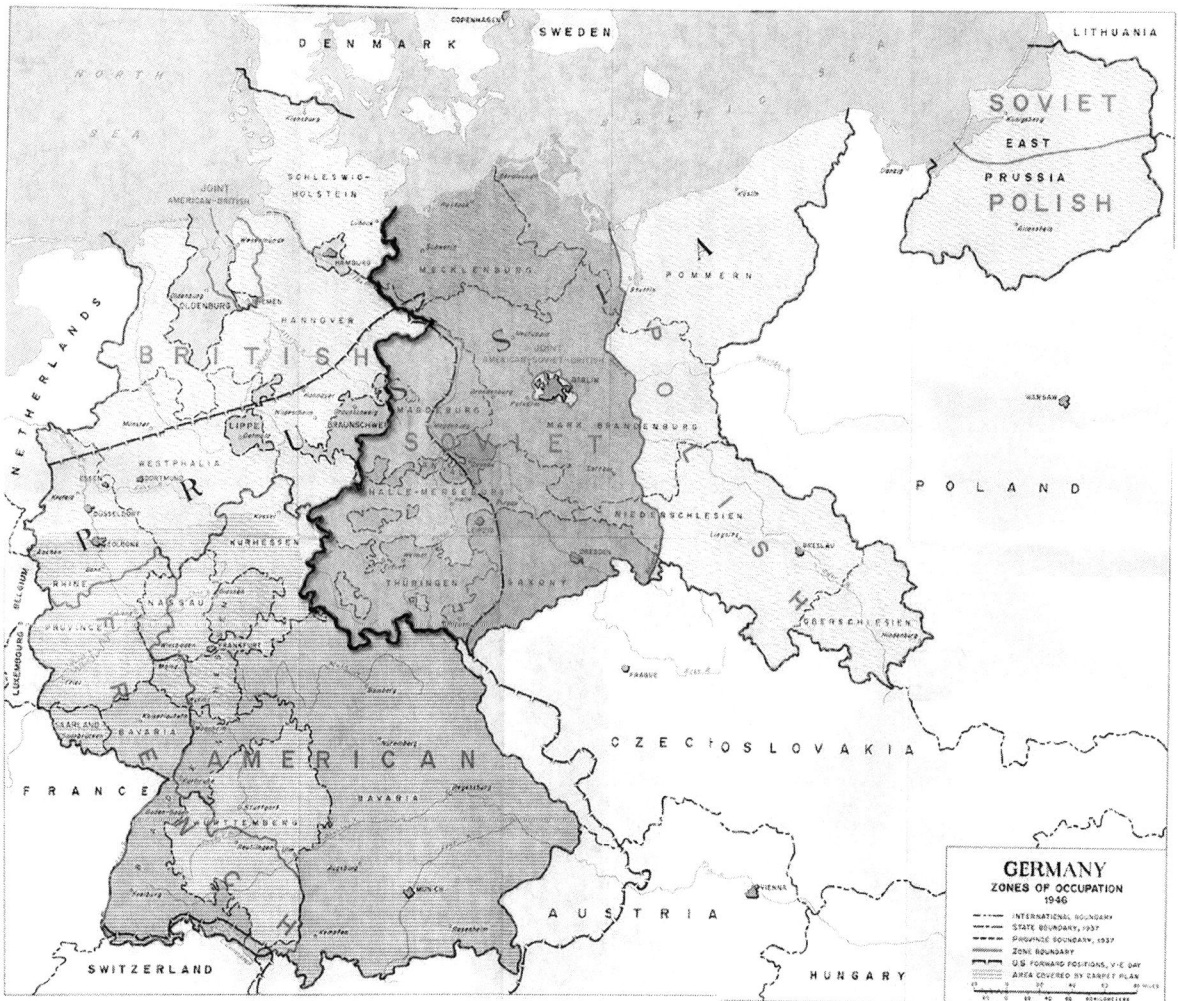

The route of the border in black

[23] David Clay Large, *Berlin* (New York: Basic Books, 2000), 425, https://www.questia.com/read/100504423.

[24] Jim Willis, Daily Life behind the Iron Curtain (Santa Barbara, CA: Greenwood, 2013), 113

Pictures of various sections of the Inner German border

In an attempt to control the people of East Berlin and avoid contact with Westerners, Ulbricht worked to isolate East Berliners. Berlin historian David Clay Large notes that by 1952, East Germany was already feeling the effects of failed agricultural collectivization schemes, extreme production quotas, the nationalization of major industry, and neglect of consumer goods. After the Inner German border's completion in 1952, East Germans could only leave for the west through the city of Berlin, but they continued to do so in droves, with over 130,000 leaving in just the second half of 1952 and the first 3 months of 1953. Ironically, instead of changing or moderating some of the demands the government was making on East German workers, Ulbricht upped production quotas to even higher levels.[25]

After West Germany regained sovereignty as an independent nation in 1955, it signed the North Atlantic Treaty and became a member of NATO. NATO member nations delivered a declaration to the effect that "They consider the government of the Federal Republic as the only German government freely and legitimately constituted and therefore entitled to speak for Germany as the representative of the German people in international affairs."[26]

Meanwhile, by 1955, East Germany was attempting to combat the "brain drain" directly through propaganda messages to the East German people. According to the Eastern Bloc, those who desired to leave the communist state were being fooled by capitalist propaganda and puppets of the western fascists:

> "In both from the moral standpoint as well as
> in terms of the interests of the whole German

---

[25] David Clay Large, *Berlin* (New York: Basic Books, 2000), 425, https://www.questia.com/read/100504423.

[26] Wilke, Manfred. The Path to the Berlin Wall: Critical Stages in the History of Divided Germany. New York: Berghahn Books, 2014.87.

nation, leaving the GDR is an act of political and moral backwardness and depravity. Those who let themselves be recruited objectively serve West German Reaction and militarism, whether they know it or not. Is it not despicable when for the sake of a few alluring job offers or other false promises about a "guaranteed future" one leaves a country in which the seed for a new and more beautiful life is sprouting, and is already showing the first fruits, for the place that favours a new war and destruction?

Is it not an act of political depravity when citizens, whether young people, workers, or members of the intelligentsia, leave and betray what our people have created through common labour in our republic to offer themselves to the American or British secret services or work for the West German factory owners, Junkers, or militarists? Does not leaving the land of progress for the morass of an historically outdated social order demonstrate political backwardness and blindness? ...[W]orkers throughout Germany will demand punishment for those who today leave the German Democratic Republic, the strong bastion of the fight for peace, to serve the deadly enemy of the

German people, the imperialists and militarists."[27]

An indication of just how bad conditions got is that the Soviets began to advise Ulbricht to ease off of collectivization and production quotas. The Soviets were becoming embarrassed by the mass defections to the west and feared that if protests were to arise in East Germany, they could spread to other communist regimes, or even the Soviet Union itself. However, for political reasons, Ulbricht refused; he had seen the results for others who had not followed a hard line approach in the past, and he believed the best way to save himself was to continue to demand more from the East German people. Thus, in defiance of the Soviets, he increased quotas by an additional 25 percent.

Finally, a group of construction workers began an informal strike that spread quickly and grew out of control in a matter of days. With the world watching, the Soviets knew they had to act quickly to leave no question about what would happen if communist authority were questioned. Soviet tanks rolled into East Berlin and the East German secret police were unleashed on the people. In the immediate clash, over 200 were killed, and almost 5,000 were arrested. The uprising, though embarrassing to the Soviets, likely guaranteed Ulbricht would remain in

---

[27] ("He Who Leaves the German Democratic Republic Joins the Warmongers", Notizbuch des Agitators ("Agitator's Notebook"), Berlin: Socialist Unity Party's Agitation Department, November 1955.

power despite his disobedience so that any appearance of "giving into protests" might be avoided.[28]

One historian sees the lack of action on the part of the various forces in Berlin as an important lesson for the USSR in the future. By not intervening in the violent response to East German protests, "what the Western Allies seemed to be saying was that the Soviets and GDR authorities had carte blanche in East Berlin, so long as they did not try to push the Western powers out of West Berlin. It was a message that the Soviets, the GDR government, and most of all the East German people, would not soon forget".[29]

From its earliest days, East Germany's economy stagnated, falling further and further behind its western neighbor, though this was not self-evident at the time. However, East Germany had a number of advantages as well, most notably the fact that it had suffered less bomb damage than the West and had a solid industrial base.

Nevertheless, supply chains the region had relied upon before the Nazis' surrender had been cut off after the war. Crucially, East Germany contained only 2% of Germany's total coal deposits.[30] It was also more sparsely populated than West Germany and the Soviet zone, and its successor

---

[28] Ibid. 429-430.
[29] Ibid.
[30] Giles MacDonogh, *After the Reich : from the fall of Vienna to the Berlin airlift* (London: John Murray, 2007), p. 202

state hemorrhaged people at shockingly high rates, seeing over 100,000 East Germans leave for the West each year during 1951, 1952, and 1953, despite the only legitimate route being the Berlin corridor.[31]

By far the most important factor in the divergence between the two countries was governance and economic management. East Germany's ruling Socialist Unity Party of Germany (SED) embarked upon five-year plans, collectivization, and central planning that proved inefficient and at times, disastrous. The productivity gap between East Germany and West Germany was evident even during the Allied division and occupation.[32]

The Cold War was punctuated by a number of rebellions in communist Central Europe and Eastern Europe, and the first took place in Berlin in June 1953, with the roots of the protests laying in failed economic plans and the gradual choking of free expression. Hardliner Walter Ulbricht had become SED Party general secretary (later termed first secretary) in 1952, and under his leadership, forced collectivization had accelerated. At the same time, the higher work quotas increased demands on workers, worsening already-difficult living standards. The latter was, by now, lagging behind the BRD, East German

---

[31] Christian Ostermann, *Uprising in East Germany, 1953 : the Cold War, the German question, and the first major upheaval behind the Iron Curtain* (Budapest: Central European Press, 2001), p. 3.

[32] Albrecht Ritschl and Tamás Vonyó, "The roots of economic failure: what explains East Germany's falling behind between 1945 and 1950?", *European Review of Economic History*, (18:2, 1 May 2014, pp. 166–184), p. 166.

citizens were experiencing shortages of essentials, and repression meant that thousands found themselves languishing in Stasi prisons.[33] Although the 1953 rebellion is remembered as a workers' uprising, it was initially aimed at the organs of the security services.[34]

After 30 years of ruling with an iron fist, Stalin died on March 5, 1953, and a battle for control ensued in Moscow. New Premier Georgy Malenkov appeared to usher in a new era of liberalization – the "New Course" – by increasing availability of consumer goods including in the DDR, and relaxing political strictures, which may have played a part in the stirring of dissent in Eastern Europe over the next three years. Angered by another increase in work quotas, Berlin construction workers nevertheless went on strike in protest on June 16, 1953, and the country-wide East German Uprising began the following day. That day, up to 372,000 workers and peasants in the countryside voiced pent-up grievances against the SED.[35] The demonstrations were brutally put-down by the communist authorities, with 21 people killed and thousands imprisoned.[36]

---

[33] Christian Ostermann, *Uprising in East Germany, 1953 : the Cold War, the German question, and the first major upheaval behind the Iron Curtain* (Budapest: Central European Press, 2001), pp. 1-3.

[34] Gary Bruce, Resistance with the people: repression and resistance in Eastern Germany, 1945 – 1955 (Oxford: Rowman & Littlefield, 2003), p. 254.

[35] Gregory R. Witkowski, "Peasants Revolt? Re-evaluating the 17 June Uprising in East Germany", *German History*, (24:2, 1 April 2006, pp. 243–266), p. 263, Mary Fulbrook, *History of Germany, 1918-2000: the divided nation* (Oxford: Blackwell, 2002), p. 155.

[36] Mary Fulbrook, *History of Germany, 1918-2000: the divided nation* (Oxford: Blackwell, 2002), p. 155.

Ulbricht's position was uncertain in June 1953, but he responded to the Uprising with repression, managing to strengthen his own position and in the process end the "New Course", with which he'd disagreed.[37] Meanwhile, the Stasi expanded its role; in addition to packing East German jails with political prisoners (estimated at 13,000, 31% of the total prison population, by 1956),[38] the security apparatus vastly increased its domestic surveillance program. Led by Minister of State for Security Erich Mielke, the Stasi sought to recruit "unofficial employees" – informants – to spy on and reduce dissent amongst the domestic civilian population.[39] It was this web of domestic spying that really marked East Germany as uniquely authoritarian and oppressive, even by the standards of contemporary regimes in Central Europe and Eastern Europe. The result was a feeling of desperation and hopelessness in the East German population,[40] exacerbated by the failure of the West to address the so-called "German Question". It was clear to DDR citizens that an SED government backed by the Soviet Union would not relax the political climate in their country, and they were to remain (at least outwardly)

---

[37] Mary Fulbrook, *History of Germany, 1918-2000: the divided nation* (Oxford: Blackwell, 2002), p. 154-157.

[38] Gary Bruce, *Resistance with the people: repression and resistance in Eastern Germany, 1945 – 1955* (Oxford: Rowman & Littlefield, 2003), p. 260.

[39] Henry Thomson, "Repression, Redistribution and the Problem of Authoritarian Control", *East European Politics and Societies*, (31: 1, 2017, pp. 68 – 92), p. 83.

[40] Gary Bruce, *Resistance with the people: repression and resistance in Eastern Germany, 1945 – 1955* (Oxford: Rowman & Littlefield, 2003), p. 255.

submissive for a further 35 years.

Mielke

As head of the SED, Ulbricht consolidated his power after the 1953 Uprising, while Moscow strengthened its support for the regime following the events in Hungary in 1956, when a revolt not unlike the one in the DDR three years earlier took hold. This time, however, Soviet tanks and soldiers occupied the country in order to restore a pliant communist government and quash the rebellion.[41]

Despite the efforts, however, the East German economy continued to deteriorate (with a slight upturn in the late 1950s) as political repression intensified.[42] The gap between the economies of West Germany and East

---

[41] Mary Fulbrook, *History of Germany, 1918-2000: the divided nation* (Oxford: Blackwell, 2002), p. 156.
[42] Ibid., p. 158

Germany had, by this time, become a chasm, and only economic reform could have reduced the need for political repression. Ulbricht was unwilling to countenance either,[43] but by the end of the 1950s, the DDR was a Stalinized police state.

The Berlin Wall

Unsurprisingly, the East Germans were in despair as far as future prospects were concerned, and increasing numbers sought migration to the West. Between 1945 and 1961, an estimated 3.5 million fled from East Germany to West Germany, while half a million moved the other way in a net emigration of three million from the DDR.[44] In 1959, 143,000 East Germans fled, and in 1960, it was 199,000. Between January and August of 1961, the figure was already 160,000.[45]

Aware of this propaganda disaster, as well as the implications of a "brain drain", SED authorities began to look for ways to prevent the exodus. At the same time, relations between the U.S. and USSR were growing more tense.

For all of his prominence and power within the Soviet Union, Nikita Khrushchev was a virtual unknown in the

---

[43] Henry Thomson, "Repression, Redistribution and the Problem of Authoritarian Control", *East European Politics and Societies*, (31: 1, 2017, pp. 68 – 92), p. 82.

[44] Mary Fulbrook, *History of Germany, 1918-2000: the divided nation* (Oxford: Blackwell, 2002), p. 158.

[45] Gary Bruce, *Resistance with the people: repression and resistance in Eastern Germany, 1945 – 1955* (Oxford: Rowman & Littlefield, 2003), p. 261.

outside world when he took power in Moscow, and the West was less than impressed to say the least. Looking at the short, heavyset Russian who wore ill-fitting suits, Khrushchev was dismissed as a buffoon. British Foreign Secretary Harold Macmillan labeled him a "fat, vulgar man" and predicted he would not last long.

However, the "buffoon" soon showed the West he was not to be trifled with. At every turn, Khrushchev took the tactic of confrontation over conciliation. A believer in the ultimate superiority of the Soviet System, Khrushchev wanted to position the Soviet Union as a player on the world stage, an equal to the Western Allies—particularly the United States. His view was summarized in a statement made to Western diplomats at the Polish Embassy in Moscow: "We will bury you." Khrushchev didn't appear to be engaging in hyperbole either; the statement came as Soviet forces were crushing an uprising in Hungary that led to the deaths of nearly 4,000 Hungarians. That said, this confrontational persona was quite at odds with how Khrushchev would later be described by a biographer ("He could be charming or vulgar, ebullient or sullen, he was given to public displays of rage (often contrived) and to soaring hyperbole in his rhetoric. But whatever he was, however he came across, he was more human than his predecessor or even than most of his foreign counterparts, and for much of the world that was enough to make the USSR seem less mysterious or menacing.").

The timeline for the wall's construction may be said to have started on November 10, 1958. After 6 years of a divided German border, Khrushchev decided to demand that West Berlin and East Berlin be united and the city become "part of the state on whose land it is situated".[46] After floating the idea in public, Khrushchev followed up with communication to his former allies in France, London, and Washington concerning his "Natural solution", but he also suggested that if Berlin were not to become a fully East German city, another acceptable solution might be reached in making West Berlin an independent "free city" under the United Nations.[47] At this time, he also issued a 6 month timeline for the city to be returned to East Germany or given "free status". According to Khrushchev, "the German Democratic Republic had scrupulously observed the stipulations of the Potsdam Agreement with regard to the eradication of militarism and liquidation of the monopolies while the Western Powers had permitted the revival of militarism and economic imperialism in the German Federal Republic".[48]

Khrushchev stepped up the pressure, particularly in the

---

[46] Ibid. 438.
[47] Ibid. 439.
[48] (State Department, 1962, p. 2). qtd. in CIA Report

U.S., believing that he could successfully use the prospect of war to convince the United States to give up its position in Berlin. U.S. ambassador Averill Harriman heard this from Khrushchev in the early summer of 1959: "We are determined to liquidate your rights in West Berlin. What good does it do for you to have eleven thousand troops in Berlin? If it came to war, we would swallow them in one gulp.... You can start a war if you like, but remember, it will be you who are starting it, not we.... West Germany knows that we could destroy it in ten minutes.... If you start a war, we may die, but the rockets will fly automatically."[49]

At the same time, Khrushchev also seemed to offer a greater openness to the West. For the first time, Khrushchev allowed American tourists to come into the country, and likewise, he allowed limited numbers of Soviet citizens to travel in the West. He was particularly interested in trade and cultural ties; since he believed in the inherent superiority of the communist system, he wanted the West to see Soviet achievements, and he also wanted Soviets to know their country was at least the equal to the West and would soon surpass it.

As a part of this opening to the West, Khrushchev was visited by then Vice President Richard M. Nixon in 1959. Nixon was the highest-ranking American official to visit

---

[49] Ibid.

the world's first Communist superpower, even though in those years, Nixon (who as president would spearhead a series of policies known as Détente that would ease the rhetoric of the Cold War) was known as a leading anti-communist who successfully led the charge against Alger Hiss. This visit became famous for the "Kitchen Debate;" In a model kitchen at the American National Exhibition in Moscow, Nixon and Khrushchev engaged in a spirited argument wherein each defended the other's economic system. Nixon's visit prompted an invitation to Khrushchev to visit the United States.

Nixon and Khrushchev

Khrushchev became the first Soviet leader to visit an

American president since the end of World War II in September 1959. For 13 days, he toured the country, fueling a media frenzy. Landing at Washington D.C. with his wife Nina Petrovna and his adult children, he proceeded to visit New York City, Los Angeles, San Francisco, Iowa, Pittsburgh, and Washington. Unfortunately for the premier, a visit to Disneyland had to be cancelled for security reasons. The trip ended with a meeting with President Eisenhower at Camp David, where the two leaders agreed to hold a summit on Berlin to settle the issues on the city. Khrushchev left the U.S. considering his visit a success, believing he had developed a strong relationship with Eisenhower, who did not feel the same way. Regardless, the president was scheduled to visit Moscow in 1960.

It was a visit that was to not to take place. On May 1, 1960 Soviet surface-to-air missiles shot down a U-2 spy plane piloted by Francis Gary Powers. The flights, which had long angered the Soviets, had been resumed after a long halt. Khrushchev held off announcing the shoot down until May 5, worried that the incident would jeopardize the summit scheduled for May 15. When the announcement was made, Khrushchev tried to blame the flights on rogue elements in the American military, trying to deflect possible blame from Eisenhower. The president, however, admitted that the flights had occurred and that he had ordered them, which put Khrushchev in a very difficult position with the summit approaching.

The Paris Summit was disaster for Khrushchev. When he arrived, he demanded an apology from Eisenhower and a promise of no more U-2 over flights. He got no apology, but Eisenhower had already suspended the flights and offered his Open Skies proposal for mutual overflight rights. Khrushchev refused, and left the summit, and Eisenhower's visit to the Soviet Union was cancelled.

The collapse of the Paris Summit ended Khrushchev's "soft approach" to the West. In his September 1960 visit to the U.N. General Assembly, he showed his "hard approach". Rather than trying to charm the West, he began the Soviet Union's wooing of the new Third-World countries in an effort to bring them into the Soviet orbit. Of course, that effort was largely forgotten by Khrushchev's personal histrionics. During a speech by a Filipino delegate criticizing the Soviet Union for decrying colonialism while engaging in it, he took off his shoe and began banging it repeatedly on his table while calling the speaker a "jerk, stooge, and lackey", and "a toady of American imperialism". When the Romanian Foreign Vice-Minister began vocally attacking the Filipino delegate, his microphone was cut off, leading to jeers among Eastern bloc members. his microphone was eventually shut off, prompting a chorus of shouts and jeers from the Eastern Bloc delegations. The meeting was immediately adjourned, with Assembly President Frederick Boland slamming his gavel down so hard that the head broke off and went flying.

Khrushchev at the United Nations in September 1960

Meanwhile, as Eisenhower's second term was coming to an end in 1960, the administration readied a military defense plan for West Berlin, even though they were loathe to put it into action and hoped that the Soviets would not take any action that would force a response. The plan included the use of nuclear warheads, and it was communicated to West German leader Adenauer that 1.5 million German casualties could be expected if it had to be put into effect.[50]

Why would the United States even consider such a response? Berlin had little strategic value to its former allies (though some spy operations had been being conducted out of and even under the city since 1945), and the city was not even particularly popular with Germans themselves. The United States had to realize that a war with the Soviets over West Berlin would be devastating and would cost lives on both sides.

The other option, however, was the one that proved to be unthinkable. In the years since the division of the city, West Berlin had become a symbol of hope against communist oppression and against the Soviet domination of Europe. The Berlin Airlift had dominated the news and

---

[50] Ibid, 440.

been reported around the world. To allow the communists to take West Berlin without a military protest would be to give silent approval to Soviet aggression and send a message to Khrushchev that his actions would be tolerated if the threat level was high enough. This could destabilize the rest of Europe as well, and the Allies had been down the road of appeasement all too recently. Eisenhower determined that he would "rather be atomized than communized".[51]

In an interesting look backward, Khrushchev's son gave a 2009 interview regarding his father's trip to America and had this to say when asked about the topic of whether or not the Berlin ultimatum was genuine: "I think it was not a bluff because it was an abnormal situation because it was two powers, or super powers, the United States and the Soviet Union. And they met, or maybe they confronted on the problem: recognition of East Berlin, or rather East Germany. For the Soviet Union, East Germany was part of the Soviet Bloc, and it was an independent country. For the United States, and the Western part of the world it was the zone of the Soviet Occupation, and it was only one Germany: West Germany. My Father tried to do everything to push Western countries for the recognition of East Germany, and he did everything. Because it was endless negotiations before that, he imposed this

---

[51] Ibid. 430-441.

ultimatum that maybe he thought he would be able to declare that in the beginning he thought that now if we recognize East Germany, then the West will recognize it, or some similar rationale. But facing the strong opposition of the West, he changed his mind, and decided that it would be too high a price to bring the confrontation to such a level, and so it was better to try to bring Americans - because it was mostly an American position, the Europeans were ready to recognize East Germany de facto - to bring them to negotiations so I would not say that it is right to call it a bluff."[52] David Large offers an assessment heard commonly amongst historians regarding the Khrushchev trip in that it made "no progress".

After the disaster of the Paris Summit and his performance at the U.N. General Assembly, Khrushchev hoped for a new beginning with the United States with the election of John F. Kennedy as the new president. Khrushchev saw Kennedy as a more likely partner in achieving an easing of tensions than the defeated Nixon, but once again, Khrushchev misjudged yet another president. What Khrushchev did not know (or if he knew, ignored) was that the new president was himself an anti-communist who had little interest in "détente" with the Soviet Union.

Kennedy's first few months in office were marked by

[52] Kyle Kordon Interview with Sergei Khrushchev 2009 GET INFO

tough talk, and within just a month of becoming President, the issue of communist Cuba became central to the Kennedy presidency. On February 3rd, 1961, President Kennedy called for a plan to support Cuban refugees in the U.S. A month later, Kennedy created the Peace Corps, a program that trained young American volunteers to help with economic and community development in poor countries. Both programs were integral pieces of the Cold War: each was an attempt to align disadvantaged groups abroad with the United State and the West, against the Soviet Union and its Communist satellites.

Cuba and the Cold War boiled over in April, when the Kennedy Administration moved beyond soft measures to direct action. From April 17-20, 1,400 CIA-trained Cuban exiles landed on the beaches of Western Cuba in an attempt to overthrow Fidel Castro. This plan, which Kennedy called the "Bay of Pigs," had been originally drafted by the Eisenhower Administration. The exiles landed in Cuba and were expected to be greeted by anti-Castro forces within the country. After this, the US was to provide air reinforcement to the rebels, and the Castro regime would slowly be overthrown.

By April 19th, however, it became increasingly clear to Kennedy that the invasion would not work. The exiles were not, as expected, greeted by anti-Castro forces. Instead, the Cuban government captured or killed all of the invaders. No U.S. air reinforcement was ever provided, flummoxing both the exiles and American military commanders. The Bay of Pigs had been an unmitigated disaster.

Unfortunately for the young president, April 1961 also witnessed the first manned space flight by Soviet cosmonaut Yuri Gagarin, handing the Soviets two propaganda victories. But the embarrassment of the failure in Cuba stiffened Kennedy's resolve not to make any concessions to the Soviets at the Vienna Summit on June 3, 1961. In their first and only face-to-face meeting (and the last meeting between a Soviet Leader and an American president until Nixon), neither man was in a mood to compromise. Khrushchev renewed his demands, but he also demanded that the U.S. withdraw all troops from West Berlin, allowing it to unite with East Berlin under GDR control. As a halfway measure, Khrushchev said he would accept Berlin as a free city without ties to the West. The leaders were also at loggerheads over an atmospheric test-ban treaty.

Khrushchev and Kennedy meet at Vienna

W.R. Smyser, author of *Kennedy and the Berlin Wall* argues that Kennedy was naive about Khrushchev's level of seriousness over the Berlin issue going into the Vienna summit because his ambassadors had not correctly communicated Khrushchev's anger and urgency on the matter. Khrushchev had told the Czechs that he planned to scare Kennedy into doing what he wanted in Berlin. He also believed humiliating Kennedy in Berlin would accomplish his further goals of causing NATO members to lose faith in the promises of the American government and scaring away Western investors from West Germany, thus leaving the country open to a takeover.[53]

---

[53] Smyser, W.R. Kennedy and the Berlin Wall. Rowman & Littlefield Publishers. 16 Sept. 2009. 59-60.

During the meeting, Khrushchev alternated between calm and, as Kennedy later described it, "going berserk". He claimed that the United States was asking the Soviet Union "to sit like schoolboy with his hands on his desk" and that since the Soviet Union believed so strongly in the ideas of communism "it [could not] guarantee that these ideas will stop at its borders".[54] Kennedy responded by explaining to Khrushchev the nature of his position on Berlin: "This matter is of the greatest concern to the U.S. We are in Berlin not because of someone's sufferance. We fought our way here, although our causalities may not have been as high as the U.S.S.R.'s. We are in Berlin not by agreement by East Germans, but by our contractual rights."[55]

Khrushchev did not react well to Kennedy's replies, alternately threatening and lecturing Kennedy that his position would lead to inevitable war between the two sides, and Smyser's discussion of Kennedy and Khrushchev suggests that Khrushchev's intimidation tactics may have worked to an extent: "Khrushchev may well have put in a show, deliberately throwing the kind of tantrums that he had thrown in some of his private meetings with MacMillan [the British Prime Minister]…An American journalist told a U.S. official that…Kennedy looked 'green' at the end of the summit.

---

[54] Ibid. 66.
[55] Large 442.

Another American wrote that Kennedy appeared 'dazed' by the 'sheer animal energy' of Khrushchev's presentation".[56]

Kennedy's performance in Vienna has met with mixed reactions. Some have put the blame for the construction of the Berlin Wall on what they see as Kennedy's weakness in his initial meeting with the Soviet premier, while others believe he more than adequately defended American sovereignty in a nearly impossible situation. At a 2011 CIA conference discussing the wall, the conference concluded that "Kennedy undercut his own bargaining position with the Soviet Premier when [he] conveyed US acquiescence to the permanent division of Berlin. This misstep in the negotiations made Kennedy's later, more assertive public statements, less credible to the Soviets, who now saw him as indecisive and weak".[57]

In a similar vein, Large discusses Kennedy's own frustration with the need to defend Berlin, indicating that Kennedy was not as committed to the city as he might have seemed in Vienna. Large recalls Kennedy's words to an aide: "We're stuck in a ridiculous position. It seems silly for us to be facing an atomic war over a treaty preserving Berlin as the future capital of a reunited Germany when all of us know that Germany will probably

---

[56] Smyser, 72.
[57] Carmichael.

never be reunited".[58] Kennedy was resolute on the point that he would not use nuclear weapons to solve the Berlin crisis or defend the city. He even indicated some understanding of Khrushchev's frustration with the large amount of East Germans leaving the country through West Berlin, and he felt that the West Germans were using the Americans for defense while they rebuilt their economy. As Kennedy expressed it, "if [the West Germans] think we are rushing into a war over Berlin, except as a last desperate move to save the NATO alliance, they've got another thing coming."[59]

Willy Brandt, the mayor of Berlin, wrote in his memoir, *My Road to Berlin*, of living as a free Berliner but with his fate being controlled largely by the decisions of the superpowers: "[T]he Allied headquarters for the present still gave the impression that the West was willing to compromise the differences by making large concessions to the Russians. Time and again the representatives of America, England, and France allowed themselves to be outmaneuvered by the Soviet side. It was the time that a spokesman of Berlin expressed the mood of many of his fellow citizens in these words: 'The worst is not that we have to fight with our backs to the wall --but that the Western powers are no wall to lean against.'"[60]

---

[58] Ibid., 443.
[59] Ibid.
[60] Willy Brandt, My Road to Berlin (Garden City, NY: Doubleday, 1960), 176, https://www.questia.com/read/55091042.

Both men left the summit empty handed, and Kennedy later told his brother Bobby that it was "like dealing with Dad. All give and no take." However, Khrushchev came away from the meeting still thinking he could push the young president around, even as the failure once again to settle the question of Berlin put the Soviet premier in a difficult situation. Though the leaders of the British, French, and American governments were convinced that the Soviets would not risk an all-out-war, Khrushchev continued to threaten that if the West did not acquiesce to his demands, the Soviets would work toward a separate peace treaty with East Germany.[61]

On June 15, 1961, Walter Ulbricht issued the following denial when asked a question in regards to a plan to separate the city: "I understand by your question that there are men in West Germany who wish that we [would] mobilize the construction workers of the GDR in order to build a wall. I don't know of any such intention. The construction workers of our country are principally occupied with home building and their strength is completely consumed by this task. Nobody has the intention of building a wall."[62] Lawrence Freedman, author of *Kennedy's Wars: Berlin, Cuba, Laos, and Vietnam*, argues that as East Germany continued to prove

---

[61] Carmichael.

[62] Lawrence Freedman, Kennedy's Wars: Berlin, Cuba, Laos, and Vietnam (New York: Oxford University Press, 2000), 72, https://www.questia.com/read/90323460.

unable to stem the tide of East Germans leaving the country through Berlin, Ulbricht attempted to "force Khrushchev's hand" by purposely dropping (and simultaneously denying) the idea of a wall or boundary being constructed in the midst of the city.[63] Other historians claim that Ulbricht had been in negotiations with Khrushchev, who was pushing for the wall and that Ulbricht's mention of it was a slip of the tongue.

Did East German leader Walter Ulbricht come to believe that the only way to avoid East Germany's demise was to construct the wall and thus seek Soviet permission to do so, or was the wall built at the behest of Nikita Khrushchev himself, anxious to press his advantage at a time when he believed the world response would be weak enough to allow him to carry out his plan without military repercussions? The answers almost surely lie in a meeting between Khrushchev and Ulbricht that took place on August 1, 1961. In a document discovered by German historian Matthias Uhl, it appears that the main impetus came from Khrushchev; the document reveals that Khrushchev had earlier broached the subject with Ulbricht through his ambassador to Berlin, sending him to "explain to him my idea of taking advantage of the current tensions with the West and laying an iron ring around Berlin". The flow of engineers out of East Germany "had to stop,"

---

[63] Ibid.

Khrushchev explained.

   In the written recording of the conversation between the two leaders, Khrushchev was the clear decision-maker, with Ulbricht's willing acquiescence. It was clear that Khrushchev was disappointed in Ulbricht's performance: "When I attended your party convention two years ago, everything was fine. What happened? You wanted to pull ahead of West Germany by 1961/62…We will give you one or two weeks to make the necessary economic preparations. Then you will convene the parliament and issue the following communiqué: 'Beginning tomorrow, checkpoints will be erected and transit will be prohibited. Anyone who wishes to cross the border can do so only with the permission of certain authorities of the German Democratic Republic.'"[64] When Ulbricht made clear to Khrushchev his desire to include his economic ministers in on the decision for the wall, Khrushchev refused, saying, "You should not explain anything before the introduction of the new border regime. It would only strengthen the flow of people leaving." If word got out about the wall construction, the Kremlin director recognized correctly, there could be "traffic jams" on Berlin's access roads. Such forms of traffic obstruction would constitute "a certain demonstration," he said.

---

[64] Wiegrefe, Klaus. "The Khrushchev Connection: Who Ordered the Construction of the Berlin Wall?". Speigel Online International. August 23, 2009.

Whatever the case, the wall's construction would begin about two months later. In the midst of negotiations, summits, and threats, East Germans continued to leave the country via Berlin at unprecedented rates. June 1961 saw approximately 19,000 leave, and July brought the exodus of another 30,000. By the 11th of August, another 16,000 were gone, and on August 12 alone, 2,400 East Germans exited the country in what would be the only legal way to do so for the next 28 years.[65] The East German parliament issued the following proclamation on August 11th, 1961: "The People's Assembly confirms the impending measures to protect the security of the GDR and to curtail the campaign of organized Kopfjägerei [head-hunting] and Menschenhandel [traffic in human lives] orchestrated from West Germany and West Berlin. The Assembly empowers the GDR Council of Ministers to undertake all the steps approved by the member states of the Warsaw Pact. The Assembly appeals to all peace-loving citizens of the GDR to give their full support to the agencies of their Workers-and-Peasants State in the application of these measures."[66]

Few would have predicted that the "impending measures" would produce the wall that would divide Berlin and the world for almost three decades, but on Sunday, August 13, East German soldiers began to install

[65] "Berlin Wall". *History.com* 2009. Web. February 11, 2015.
[66] Ibid. 446.

posts and connect barbed wire to seal off the eastern part of the city.

East Germans sealing the border and installing barbed wire on August 13

What caused the wall to be built on the 13th rather than another day? Permission for the barbed wire portion of the wall had been granted on August 5th, and Large argues that several signs from the Americans gave Khrushchev the impression that the United States would not take action if the wall was constructed. The remarks of American Senator William Fulbright were also seen by many as an encouragement to Khrushchev. On an ABC news show on July 30th, 1961, Fulbright discussed the heavy losses of man and brainpower being experienced by East Germany and remarked, "I don't understand why the

East Germans don't close their border, because I think they have a right to close it."[67]

In fact, Khrushchev himself gave direct orders to the East Germans constructing the wall that the initial attempt at a barrier be made only with wire and fence posts to test the West's response. When none was forthcoming, he gave the go-ahead for concrete block walls to be put into place beginning on the 15th of August.

The construction of the wall on August 15

All told, the wall itself was constructed by 32,000 East

[67] Jack Kenny, "The Wall, Hiding Shame: The Berlin Wall Was Erected in 1961 to Stop the Continual Flight of East Germans to the West, Owing to the Abject Failure of Collectivism in the Soviet-Bloc Country," The New American, August 22, 2011, https://www.questia.com/read/1G1-265977875.

German engineers with materials that had been collected over a multiple months in preparation for the divide.[68] In an article in *Antiquity*, Frederick Baker seeks to change misconceptions about the wall that he believes exist because of the tourism generated by pieces of the wall after 1989. Baker explains, "'The Wall' was a set of in-depth border fortifications that consisted of two parallel walls: an interior and an exterior one enclosed a 'death strip' and watch-towers".[69] The interior wall was more of a makeshift border control that involved the use of barbed wire, abandoned buildings, and even small bodies of water.

Baker also set forth the four phases of construction of the wall that separated East and West Berliners from each other for 28 years. The first phase of the wall was initially constructed of wire, fence posts, and chipped cobblestone from the surrounding streets and the surrounding of the city was complete by the afternoon of August 14th. Reinforced sections of concrete were added to this when the Soviets become assured that the West would not attempt to remove the original wire barriers. Though Baker describes the first phase of the wall as "flimsy", he admits that it was largely effective at stemming the tide of East Germans leaving the country.[70]

---

[68] John S. Brown, "The Erstwhile Berlin Wall at 50," Army, August 2011, https://www.questia.com/read/1P3-2413938141.

[69] Frederick Baker, "The Berlin Wall: Production, Preservation and Consumption of a 20th-Century Monument," Antiquity 67, no. 257 (1993), https://www.questia.com/read/1G1-15143722.

There were issues with the wall, especially along the Bernauer Strasse, where occupied residences actually made up part of the construction and people could walk or jump their way to the west. Furthermore, underground trains could still travel underneath the wall, as long as no stops were made in East Berlin. After the East Germans determined that the potential (and actual) escapes were too great of a risk, they bulldozed the homes along the Bernauer Strasse, built an exterior wall on the other side of it, and created what would become known as the "death strip".[71]

---

[70] Ibid.

[71] Mark Ehrman, "Borders and Barriers," The Virginia Quarterly Review 83, no. 2 (2007), https://www.questia.com/read/1P3-1256577881.

Pictures of the death strip

The second phase of the wall was all concrete, with smooth pipe at the top in most sections. This wall was more permanent and impressive, as well as more secure since it included 260 guard towers. This section included embedded flares ready to go off, trip wires lying under the sand that surrounded the guard tower road, dogs ready to chase down and attack potential escapees, and 5 inch spikes designed to impale the feet or bodies of any who attempted to jump from the top of the wall. The division of the city was so important to the East that even the sewage system that lay underneath the city was secured.[72]

In 1976, a third version of the wall was begun, and this is
the one that most people remember since it was in
existence when the wall came down in 1989. Though
under public pressure, some of the more flagrant
"defenses" were no longer a part, but it's important not to
discount the huge psychological effect the massive final
version of the wall had on those contemplating the
"crime" of leaving East Germany: "The symbolic
discouragement should not be exaggerated in comparison
with the physical: the order to shoot, in operation on the

[72] Baker.

border since the 1950s, became a part of the official constitution in May 1982".[73]

In conjunction with the Berlin Wall was the Inner German Wall, stretching over 870 miles, dividing East Germany from West Germany, and guarded on the eastern side by frontier troops known as *Grentztruppen*.[74]

Many observers of the days and nights following August 13th would be witness to divided couples, friends, and business partners separated by the wall that seemed to appear out of nowhere. Norman Gelb, who was the Mutual Broadcasting System correspondent in Berlin at the time of the building of the wall, was allowed to enter East Germany during the immediate days after August 13th when the Soviets were still allowing foreign nationals to cross the border between East and West Berlin somewhat freely. He recalls one of the most poignant scenes being East Germans who had packed their things and made it to the border between the cities, only to find that they had been sealed into East Germany. Compounding that misfortune was the fact that as they made their way back to their homes, they knew they had exposed themselves to the East German Secret Police.[75]

[73] Ibid.
[74] Rottman, Gordon. The Berlin Wall and the Inner German Border 1961-1989, New York: Osprey Publishing, 2008,4.
[75] Norman Gelb, "The Wall That Shut out the West," The Christian Science Monitor, August 14, 1996, https://www.questia.com/read/1P2-33414015.

The construction of the wall not only separated families and friends but also instilled fear among the German leadership in the west. Some of the concern was based on the hope that West Berliners would not partake in any violence against the soldiers and party members constructing the wall, which might provide an excuse for an East German or Soviet attack on West Berlin itself. Kennedy, however, did not fear such an attack. As he saw it, "Why would Khrushchev put up a wall if he really intended to seize West Berlin? There shouldn't be any need of a wall if he occupied the whole city. This is his way out of his predicament. It's not a nice solution, but a wall is a hell of a lot better than a war".[76]

Of course, not everyone, least of all West Berliners, appreciated Kennedy's take on the new wall that divided their city. As the wall was going up, Brandt complained, "The Berlin Senate publicly condemns the illegal and inhuman measures being taken by those who are dividing Germany. The cold concrete stakes that cut through our city have been driven into the heart of German unity and into the living organism of our single city of Berlin". Three days later, Brandt heavily criticized Kennedy in writing for his lack of response, saying of the wall's ongoing construction, "I think this is a serious turning point in the post-war history of the city as it has not been

[76] Ibid., 452.

seen since the blockade. The development has not changed the resistance or will of the people of West Berlin, but it was likely to raise doubts in the reaction ability and determination of the three powers… Inactivity and pure defensiveness could cause a crisis of confidence with the Western powers. I consider the situation serious enough, Mr. President, to write to you in all frankness as is possible only between friends who trust each other completely…"[77]

Kennedy was angered by Brandt's letter, but he did send Vice President Lyndon Johnson and General Lucius Clay (who had orchestrated the Berlin Airlift) to help reassure Berliners that the United States had not abandoned them. On August 19th, Johnson delivered a speech to the welcoming crowds that had gathered in West Berlin, promising, "To the survival and to the creative future of this city we Americans have pledged, in effect, what our ancestors pledged in forming the United States—'our lives, our fortunes, and our sacred honor.' The President wants you to know and I want you to know that the pledge he has given to the freedom of West Berlin and to the rights of Western access to Berlin is firm.... This island does not stand alone."[78]

Some Germans believed that the United States had failed

[77] "Brief des Regierenden Bürgermeisters von Berlin, Willy Brandt, an den amerikanischen Präsidenten John F. Kennedy" 16. August 1961. *Chronik der Mauer*. Translated from the German.
[78] Large, 455.

to protect Germany, claiming that they could and should have prevented the building of the wall in the months leading up to August 13th. Those who hold to this position would argue that since the West had initially acted as administrators in the division of Berlin and Germany, had put such severe limitations on the military development of West Germany, and entered into NATO alliance with it, the building of the wall can be laid at the feat of a United States for acting ambiguously instead of directly.[79]

However, in her 1967 book *The Wall is Not Forever*, Eleanor Dulles explains that while the nine weeks that followed Kennedy and Khrushchev's meetings were characterized with concern over the next move of the Soviets, the idea of an actual wall of separation being constructed was not taken seriously. Despite the flurry of speculation about the fallout of Kennedy and Khrushchev's discussion, German newspapers were not speculating on a physical division of the city. Dulles quotes one German as remembering, "In no West Berlin newspaper was the possibility of a total control and eventual [counter] measures seriously discussed.... No one believed that the regime would go as far as to take the measures for a complete sealing off."[80] It was, however,

---

[79] Eleanor Lansing Dulles, *Berlin: The Wall Is Not Forever* (Chapel Hill, NC: University of North Carolina Press, 1967), 49, https://www.questia.com/read/30327334.
[80] Ibid.

the general opinion in East Germany that American equivocation on their position on Berlin meant that East Germans who wanted to leave their country before it was too late needed to do so immediately. This led to an increase in emigrations that threatened the viability of East German factories, agriculture, and even the survival of the East German state.[81]

Once the wall was constructed, anger was unleashed at both the Soviets and the Americans. In remembrance of Neville Chamberlain's appeasement of the Nazis in Munich in the years leading to World War II, Berlin schoolchildren sent John F. Kennedy a black umbrella.[82] This was ironic since Khrushchev tried to distance himself from the wall to an extent, even as he did not want to lose the impression that he was taking a hard line against the West. In a conversation with the ambassador to West Germany, he explained, "I wouldn't want to conceal from you that it was I who in the last instance gave the order for it...I know that the Wall is an ugly thing. It will also disappear. However only when the reasons for its construction have gone'".[83]

Though Khrushchev was interested in Berlin in the long term, the mass exodus of young people from a country already faced with production and technological deficits

[81] Ibid. 51.
[82] Large, 452.
[83] Ruhle & Holzwei qtd. in Baker.

was the immediate concern of the Soviet premier: "What was I supposed to do? More than 30,000 people, the best and most capable of the country, left the GDR in July. It is quite easy to calculate the moment of breakdown of the East German economy if we had not done something to stop the mass flight. There were only two alternatives: an air transport blockade, or the Wall. The former would have caused trouble with the USA which might have led to war. I could not and did not want to risk this. Therefore, the Wall was the only solution."[84]

Public relations were, ironically, very important to Soviet-controlled East Germany in the years that followed the creation of the wall (when the largest amount of escape attempts were made). The Soviets were aware that walling off of a city could not look positive to the parts of the world in which they did not control the press, but they insisted on "anti-fascist rampart" rhetoric despite this fact. When people attempting to cross the border were killed, therefore, the "corpse cases" that resulted were to be handled by the Stasi, the East German secret police. Bodies were transported to medical facilities or universities for autopsy and study. Those injured in an attack were transported by army vehicles rather than ambulances, and they were sent to hospitals further away for the prying eyes of the press rather than to the closest

[84] Mark Ehrman, "Borders and Barriers," The Virginia Quarterly Review 83, no. 2 (2007), https://www.questia.com/read/1P3-1256577881.

hospitals where a person might get the best or most immediate care.[85]

Of course, those outside of the Eastern Bloc things saw things far differently. Shortly before the fall of the Berlin wall in 1989, an American named Gerald Kelinfeld spoke in West Berlin about what the wall symbolized to Americans: "For the Americans, the wall is a symbol of injustice, of inhumanity, of disrespect for human rights; perhaps it is more important than for some West Germans and West Berliners…The United States is here because of national interests, but also because of political ideals. This is precisely the point. Every American administration advocates the right of the German people to self-determination. Public support is broad and deep. When the wall turned twenty-five, even provincial newspapers in the United States contained comprehensive coverage of the history and significance of this monument."[86]

At the time of the wall's construction, however, the West was taken somewhat by surprise. In retrospect, some have asked if the United States should have committed troops to Berlin to stop the construction of the massive wall that divided families for 28 years. These wonder if, at the point of the wall's origin, when it was still more of a threat than a reality, its permanency could have been

---

[85] Ibid.
[86] Wilke, Manfred. The Path to the Berlin Wall: Critical Stages in the History of Divided Germany. New York: Berghahn Books, 2014.

avoided: "The frail strands of wire and wooden booms manned by soldiers in August 13 and 14, with only a few cement and stone obstructions, could have been breached. There were even a few crossing points open, but the separation probably could not have been thwarted except in terms of a major contest between the United States and the USSR."

Either way, it's clear that the United States was not ready to take on that major contest in 1961. On August 13th, Secretary of State Dean Rusk informed John F. Kennedy that the wall was being built, yet Kennedy continued with his plans to go sailing in Hyannis Port.[87] That makes clear that the administration was not even considering military action against the East Germans or Soviets, although they would condemn the action. As Khrushchev had predicted in 1959, "The leaders of the United States are not such idiots as to fight over Berlin."[88]

Moreover, the leaders of France and Britain, Charles DeGaulle and Harold McMillan, showed even less concern over the initial construction of the wall. Neither leader immediately returned to their capital to address the situation. Both countries had their militaries and budgets committed to other places in the world, and neither believed that the people they had worked so hard to defeat

---

[87] Yosefa Loshitzky, "Constructing and Deconstructing the Wall," *CLIO* 26, no. 3 (1997), https://www.questia.com/read/1G1-19984489.

[88] David Clay Large, *Berlin* (New York: Basic Books, 2000), https://www.questia.com/read/100504423.

only 15 years ago were worth defending to the death simply because their city was divided.[89]

The successful construction of the wall surprised not only the West but the East as well. Since the East Germans and Soviets were fully aware that the West had several options to stop construction, in the initial stages simply by removing physical barriers, making use of the uniformed reserve troops that Kennedy ordered to Berlin in the aftermath, or even by the use of nuclear weapons against the East Germans, they were emboldened when they found there would be little response. Thus, in the months that followed construction of the initial wall and border, harassment of allied officials crossing into East Berlin began to become regular. At checkpoints Alpha and Bravo, guards began interfering in the "unhindered access" of Western officials into East Berlin, which was a clear violation of the 1945 agreements between the powers.

In 2011, the Cold War International History Project issued a report after investigating the circumstances of almost 600 deaths at, near, or involving the Berlin Wall to provide and accurate accounting of the number of deaths caused by "either an attempted escape or a temporal and

---

[89] "The Berlin Wall: A Secret History: The Berlin Wall Was a Tangible Symbol of the Suppression of Human Rights by the Eastern Bloc during the Cold War, but Frederick Taylor Asks Whether It Was More Convenient to the Western Democracies Than Their Rhetoric Suggested," History Today, February 2007, https://www.questia.com/read/1G1-159921707.

spatial link between the death and the border regime".[90]
The report features explanations of how many of those
who tried to cross either the wall or the Inner German
border died, as well as how their deaths were handled by
the East Germans. In addition to that, in only a few
months, the East German government had over 10,000
political prisoners, which were very expensive to keep in
confinement. It was at this time that the East German
government contacted their counterparts about the
possibility of West Germany purchasing political
prisoners. The rationale provided was that the East was
losing their education investment with every young person
that left the GDR, and over the years of the wall's
existence, West German did negotiate the purchase of
release for many who were captured attempting to flee the
East.[91]

It is difficult to make generalizations about those who
escaped East Germany between 1961 and 1989. This
group would include the young and old, males and
females, and everyday citizens as well as soldiers and
officials. In attempting to find some commonalities
among the little over 40,000 who escaped East Germany,
one can point to youth, those who were separated from
relatives or spouses in the West, those who desired

[90] Hertle, Hans-Hermann and Maria Nooke. "The Victims at the Berlin Wall, 1961-1989". *Cold War International History Project.* August 2011.
[91] Large, 459.

freedom for their children, and people angry at the surveillance state that the Stasi had created in East Germany.

Almost half of the 40,000 made their escape in the first four years of the wall's existence,[92] a time when East Germans were still experiencing the shock and desperation of separation and the chances of successful escape were higher. As the information the Stasi collected on escapees grew, they adjusted security measures accordingly.

Measures of escape went from the imaginative, such as using hot air balloons, a homemade plane constructed from the parts of a Trabant automobile, an armor-plated car, or a crossing by wires, to the more conventional methods of simply walking across the border through one of the checkpoints with falsified documents. Of course, in any type of escape, the event was never mundane; all escapees risked their lives and at times, the lives or safety of anyone the Stasi discovered was a part of the plan to escape. After an East German ferry boat was "hijacked" by a few Berliners and successfully made it to a drop off point in West Berlin, East German passenger ships had their steering wheels removed each night and demoted its former captain to a freight worker.[93]

---

[92] Willis, 114-115.
[93] Wilis, 118.

Some 13 tunnels were created underneath the city of Berlin, connecting escapees to freedom, but not without danger of cave-ins or being discovered. One of the most successful tunnels was dug by a group of students who had escaped to West Berlin, and this tunnel was responsible for the successful escape of 57 East Germans before its existence was betrayed to a member of the Stasi. It is interesting to note how many escape stories end in this note, but whatever the reasons, the Stasi were quite successful in rooting out plans to escape and at following leads provided by those who had been left behind. They were perhaps most successful at infiltrating groups or organizations where escape might be a topic of discussion.

Struggling to Secure Legitimacy

Securing the DDR's borders and stemming the loss of labor and skills gave the SED increased confidence to try out new domestic policies. Whereas First Secretary Ulbricht had been resistant to liberalization in the 1950s, he now realized that the lack of material progress was undermining socialist rule, and by the early 1960s, a debate took was taking place within the communist world, including the Soviet Union, over how to reform their moribund economies.[94] The issue was particularly acute in the DDR, where progress could be directly compared with the *Wirtschaftswunder* in West Germany. The relative

---

[94] Ibid, p. 164.

economic advancement of the two states was an indictment of centrally-planned socialism and a great advertisement for liberal capitalism. The BRD had been transformed from rubble into an export-driven, prosperous society within a short period of time, while the DDR was particularly lacking in consumer goods, with shops containing a single variety of most items and often experiencing shortages. "Luxury" goods, such as the DDR-produced Trabant car (known as "Trabi" to Germans), required "consumers" to sit on a waiting list, depending on their proximity to Berlin and their SED party contacts, which could stretch out over a period of many months or even years.

This realization may have served, partly, as justification for the *Neues Ökonomisches System* (New Economic System) introduced by Ulbricht in 1963. The NÖS contained a number of mildly liberalizing measures intended to improve growth and material progress, allowing for some degree of entrepreneurship and incentivizing, as well as a more liberal approach to music and literature.[95] It is difficult to assess how successful the program actually was due to its relatively short implementation period. It is possible that it could have transformed the economic fortunes of the DDR and its

---

[95] Andrew Evans, "The Last Gasp of Socialism: Economics and Culture in 1960s East Germany", *German Life and Letters*, (63, 2010, pp. 331–344), p. 332, Mary Fulbrook, *History of Germany, 1918-2000: the divided nation* (Oxford: Blackwell, 2002), pp. 164-165.

citizens, but the policy was gradually abandoned at the end of the 1960s. This was, in part, because of events in Czechoslovakia, where the Prague Spring – a social and economic liberalization dubbed "socialism with a human face" - was brutally rubbed out by an invasion of Warsaw Pact forces in August 1968.[96] A similar pattern of protest and crackdown occurred in Poland in 1970. In addition, hardliners in the ruling SED in East Germany had not been overly supportive of the policy in the first place,[97] and it was clear to others in the communist bloc that Moscow would not tolerate significant economic liberalization.

As well as material progress, the SED regime of the 1960s faced a recurring problem over how to achieve recognition from the rest of the world. Since its foundation in 1949, most countries had refused to recognize the DDR, shutting it out of international institutions like the United Nations (UN). This issue was compounded by the official policy of the BRD. Walter Hallstein, at the West German Foreign Ministry, had stated in 1955 that any country maintaining diplomatic relations with the DDR (with the exception of the Soviet Union itself) would be considered persona non grata in Bonn. What came to be known as the "Hallstein Doctrine"

---

[96] Konrad H. Jarausch and Helga A. Welsh, "Two Germanies, 1961-1989", German History in Documents and Images (German Historical Institute: http://germanhistorydocs.ghi-dc.org/, [accessed 6 October 2017], p. 4.

[97] Mary Fulbrook, *History of Germany, 1918-2000: the divided nation* (Oxford: Blackwell, 2002), p. 166.

implied that the West Germany would refuse to recognize any country that recognized East Germany, part of a wider campaign to isolate the East Germans in the 1950s and 1960s.[98] The DDR was constantly seeking legitimacy during this period but ultimately, most countries decided that between East Germany and West Germany, they were more willing to offend the former rather than the latter, which demonstrates the constant insecurity of the state. In addition to being isolated by the West, it was given only limited autonomy by the Soviets, and it was ostracized or ignored by much of the world. It is perhaps unsurprising, then, that the DDR regime adopted a siege mentality for much of its existence.

Part of the SED's strategy for legitimacy involved supporting liberation movements in the newly decolonized countries of Africa.[99] This foreign policy satisfied two broad goals by acting as a proxy for Soviet interests and expanding the number of countries sympathetic to the DDR, thereby increasing its legitimacy. For instance, Ulbricht visited Gamal Abdul Nasser in Egypt in 1965,[100] forging an African link that would deepen over coming years, known in the DDR as *Afrikapolitik*.[101] Nevertheless, SED leadership still

---

[98] William Glenn Gray, *Germany's Cold War: The Global Campaign to Isolate East Germany, 1949-1969* (London: University of North Carolina Press, 2003), p. 223.

[99] Gareth M. Winrow, *The Foreign Policy of the GDR in Africa* (Cambridge: Cambridge University Press, 1990)

[100] Ibid, p. 113.

[101] Ibid, p. 225.

suffered numerous humiliations when post-colonial leaders canceled planned visits to Berlin.[102]

Another part of this strategy hinged on Olympic success. Training programs for DDR athletes marked a particularly troubling segment of the country's history. Many Olympic athletes were subjected to forced doping without their consent or knowledge, which reaped short-term rewards on the track but left many competitors with long-lasting physiological problems.[103] This was probably not what Ulbricht had meant when he'd articulated the DDR's idea of *Abgrenzung,* outlining how the people of East Germany had a unique, "demarcated" character, different than their brethren in the West.[104]

Ironically, the outlook for the DDR improved at the end of the 1960s with the assistance of West Germany itself, a most unexpected source of support. But Willy Brandt's policy of rapprochement is considered by many to be the beginning of the end of the SED regime, as it struggled to survive under the weight of its own contradictions.

West German politics had been dominated by the center-right CDU/CSU (Christian Democratic Party and its Bavarian affiliate the Christian Social Union) coalition since the late 1940s. The center-left SPD (Social

---

[102] William Glenn Gray, *Germany's Cold War: The Global Campaign to Isolate East Germany, 1949-1969* (London: University of North Carolina Press, 2003), p. 222.
[103] Ibid, p. 220.
[104] Ibid, p. 232.

Democratic Party) had abandoned its Marxist heritage in the late 1950s, moving toward greater electoral credibility under Brandt's leadership. A one-time mayor of West Berlin, Brandt had opposed the Nazi regime, fled persecution to Norway in 1933, and had fought against German forces during World War II. In the 1966 election, his SPD did well enough to enter into a "Grand Coalition" with the CDU and lead a governing coalition from 1969. Brandt was also the first foreign minister and chancellor, in possession of a moral authority, that rarest of attributes in a post-war German politician when so many of them had Nazi pasts.[105]

Brandt and his closest colleagues–such as Egon Bahr–reasoned that West Germany's approach to the communist world, including the DDR, had reaped few results by the late 1960s, so he pursued better relations with his eastern neighbors through dialogue, ultimately settling unresolved questions dating back to 1945. *Ostpolitik* shocked the world, and it also surprised Ulbricht and the SED. Brandt met with DDR Prime Minister Willi Stoph in the East German city of Erfurt in March 1970, subsequently signing treaties with the Soviet Union and Poland later that year.[106]

In 1972, the two states signed the "Basic Treaty", each

---

[105] Mary Fulbrook, *History of Germany, 1918-2000: the divided nation* (Oxford: Blackwell, 2002), p. 169.
[106] Ibid.

recognizing the sovereignty of the other. The West Germans had apparently accepted a permanent division with the DDR, and Brandt had seemingly abandoned the Hallstein Doctrine. With that, both countries were admitted to the UN in 1973. The East Germans saw better relations with the West as a means to finally achieve legitimacy, as well as to increase trade in goods and reduce indebtedness by obtaining much-needed, hard currency.[107]

The process of *Ostpolitik* appeared to be complete by 1975, when the countries of Europe, as well as the US and USSR, signed the Helsinki Final Act, a treaty recognizing the continent's post-war borders, a long-term objective of the SED. By this point, both East Germany and West Germany (now led by Willy Brandt's successor, Helmut Schmidt) signed the Helsinki accords. Nevertheless, within the document lay the treaty's so-called "third basket", containing human rights provisions, strongly supported by the West Germans. It is a bizarre fact that oppressive regimes such as the DDR and the Soviet Union signed this document. It may have been that the communist countries had considered it a minor detail they were willing to ignore in return for credibility on the world stage. Many historians, however, consider this to be another chink in the authoritarian armor of the Iron

[107] M.E. Sarotte, *Dealing with the Devil : East Germany, Detente, and Ostpolitik, 1969-1973,* (The University of North Carolina Press, 2001), p. 164.

Curtain, because before long, dissidents in Czechoslovakia and others in Central Europe and Eastern Europe were citing Helsinki in their demands for democratic reform.[108] In the DDR, a growing number of dissidents also emerged, and while the Stasi did its utmost to monitor and stifle them, increased contact with the West caused mass disillusionment with the SED regime over its inability to deliver on the promises of material improvement.[109]

Ostpolitik was difficult for both sides. Under heavy pressure from conservatives at home, Brandt and Bahr felt squeamish about dealing with Ulbricht, whom they saw as a dictator.[110] The SED, for their part, viewed West Germany as a degenerate capitalist power.[111] At the same time, *Ostpolitik* worried allies on both sides. National Security Advisor Henry Kissinger was concerned that *Ostpolitik* would bring the two sides closer together and act as the stimulus to revive German nationalism,[112] while the Soviets fretted the DDR was acting too independently and could be incorporated into the Western sphere of influence.

---

[108] Gerald Knaus, 'Europe and Azerbaijan: The End of Shame', *Journal of Democracy*, (26:3, July 2015, pp. 5-18)

[109] Konrad H. Jarausch and Helga A. Welsh, "Two Germanies, 1961-1989", German History in Documents and Images (German Historical Institute: http://germanhistorydocs.ghi-dc.org/, [accessed 6 October 2017], p. 9.

[110] M.E. Sarotte, *Dealing with the Devil : East Germany, Detente, and Ostpolitik, 1969-1973,* (The University of North Carolina Press, 2001), p. 164.

[111] Ibid.

[112] Niall Ferguson, *Kissinger 1923-1968: The Idealist* (London: Allen Lane, 2015), p. 703.

As a result, Ulbricht was deposed in 1971 and replaced by the apparently more pliable Erich Honecker, who, nevertheless, pursued a virtually identical policy.[113] A communist since his youth, he was a hardliner who had long been a proponent of a "shoot to kill" policy for people who tried to escape across the border. Honecker had been a favorite of Ulbricht's, but now the apprentice had acted, with Soviet connivance, to depose his master.[114]

---

[113] M.E. Sarotte, *Dealing with the Devil : East Germany, Detente, and Ostpolitik, 1969-1973,* (The University of North Carolina Press, 2001), p. 168

[114] Konrad H. Jarausch and Helga A. Welsh, "Two Germanies, 1961-1989", German History in Documents and Images (German Historical Institute: http://germanhistorydocs.ghi-dc.org/, [accessed 6 October 2017], p. 4.

Honecker

Critics of *Ostpolitik* denigrated Brandt for making concessions to the East without gaining anything in return, save increased visitor rights for separated family members. They neglected to realize that by agreeing to talks, the SED had acknowledged its own weakness.[115] The West Germans' embrace of the DDR during *Ostpolitik* may have seemed questionable at the time but increased contact between the two states actually served to further delegitimize the communist system and the SED regime.

With the NÖS discarded and citizens increasingly able to see the affluence of the West, it was left to the Stasi to pacify the DDR population. At its peak, the Stasi is believed to have employed (or coerced into action) 1 informant out of every 6.5 East German citizens.[116]

Ostpolitik and the 1972 Basic Treaty did not mean the two states were completely stable in that period. A number of protests had erupted in West Germany in 1967 and 1968, part of the student unrest that had swept Europe and the United States, and the so-called "New Left" was a potent force in the West. As a result, there was a short-lived ideological convergence between activists in West

---

[115] M.E. Sarotte, *Dealing with the Devil : East Germany, Detente, and Ostpolitik, 1969-1973,* (The University of North Carolina Press, 2001), p. 170.

[116] Paul H Robinson, Sarah M. Robinson, *Pirates, Prisoners, and Lepers: Lessons from Life Outside the Law*, (University of Nebraska Press, 2015), p. 156.

Berlin and their compatriots in the east of the city.[117]
Some radicals on the New Left would form the *Rote Armee Fraktion* (Red Army Faction), a more sinister group that was responsible for committing terrorist acts for almost 20 years.

Consolidating the State at Home and Abroad

In the mid-1970s, East Germany had its best opportunity to consolidate itself domestically and on the world stage: the DDR had finally gained the recognition it sought after decades in geopolitical limbo, trade links with the West after the 1972 Basic Treaty had brought in desperately needed hard currency and goods, and the international environment had entered a more benign phase. Superpower détente had eased tensions between the United States and the Soviet Union, Berlin had moved off the world's front pages, and a generation that had only experienced socialism was emerging in the DDR. Unfortunately for East Germans, the country was not blessed with far-sighted leaders and Honecker was a prime example of this.

Born in 1912, Honecker had devoted his whole life to the communist cause. Imprisoned by the Nazis, a stalwart of the young communists, Honecker had risen meteorically within the SED ranks. He was the architect behind the

---

[117] Anna von der Goltz, "Attraction and Aversion in Germany's '1968': Encountering the Western Revolt in East Berlin", *Journal of Contemporary History*, (50:3, 2014, pp. 536 – 559), p. 558.

construction of the Berlin Wall and had pushed out Ulbricht in 1971. For all that, however, Honecker apparently had no conception of the humanistic underpinnings of socialism; he was considered ruthless and selfish, and he was promoted consistently due to the lack of viable alternatives.[118]

The Basic Treaty did not end Honecker's feeling of insecurity, and he expanded upon policies that aimed at improving the DDR's legitimacy.[119] Most callously, this involved the institutionalization of the Olympic doping program, whose results stunned the world with 20 gold medals at the Munich games in 1972, 40 in Montreal in 1976, and 47 in Moscow in 1980. In each of these games, the DDR finished an astonishing second on the medals leaderboard. Inevitably, it was not long before foreign observers began to grow suspicious of the East German authorities and their training regimens.

Honecker's other great concern was the East German economy. He oversaw the development of the *Kombinate* system, essentially a collection of state-owned and guided enterprises and industries, doing his best to completely crush private enterprise until the end of the 1970s (when the world economy went into a renewed slump).[120] This

---

[118] David Wilsford, *Political Leaders of Contemporary Western Europe: A Biographical Dictionary* (Westport, Connecticut: Greenwood, 1995), p. 199.
[119] David Wilsford, *Political Leaders of Contemporary Western Europe: A Biographical Dictionary* (Westport, Connecticut: Greenwood, 1995), p. 197.
[120] Ibid.

was the great age of communist functionaries, and Honecker perfectly encapsulated the leaders of the Eastern bloc communist parties in the 1970s and 1980s: bureaucratic, essentially incompetent, and unable to comprehend policies that might entail reform. In the end, it would be Honecker who would lead the state to its final demise.

Honecker also sought to expand upon the state's foray into the developing world. Known in the parlance of the time as the "Third World" (as potentially not capitalist or communist, although later, this came to signify poorer regions), Honecker had several objectives when it came to foreign policy. The SED government wanted to improve its access to trade, raw materials, and hard currency in its overseas strategy, goals all partially met by Honecker's trips abroad.[121] Typically, these visits included meetings with leaders in newly decolonized countries, with "freedom fighters," and recent or potential converts to the communist cause. Honecker met with Colonel Gaddafi in Libya and other left-wing or nationalist fellow travelers in Angola, Mozambique, Tanzania, and Ethiopia.[122] In this respect, the DDR's approach was similar to Cuba's in its support for left-wing regimes, as Cuba had supported communists militarily in Angola and others over many

[121] Gareth M. Winrow, *The Foreign Policy of the GDR in Africa* (Cambridge: Cambridge University Press, 1990), p. 221.
[122] Ibid, p. 113.

years. The DDR also offered incentives to African governments, including vocational, technical, and journalist training for Africans for several months in East Germany itself.[123] The SED also supplied weapons and military assistance to groups from the African National Congress in South Africa to the Zimbabwe African National Union (ZANU) and the South West Africa People's Organization (SWAPO) in Namibia.[124] This foreign policy activity reflected a rare moment in Cold War history when the communist world seemed to be in its ascendancy. This was reflected in the growing confidence of Honecker's moves overseas.

In a more benign international environment, the 1970s represented a chance for the SED government to focus on economic development. Despite earlier criticisms of Ulbricht and Honecker's leadership, both were acutely aware that the East German economy was key to the regime's survival. Although the DDR never compared favorably to its West German neighbor, by the standards of the communist world, it was more economically successful. The genesis of a trading relationship between East and West in the DDR is evidenced by East Germany's use as a source of cheap labor for products sold in the East. In addition, and more troublingly, the

---

[123] Deutsche Welle, "Africa and communist East Germany", [accessed 18 October 2017], http://www.dw.com/en/africa-and-communist-east-germany/g-18753769
[124] Ibid.

DDR exploited its prison population as forced labor in order to make the goods it needed to export in exchange for hard currency.[125]

Persistent Problems

By the 1980s, despite the continued specter of the Stasi, the citizens of the DDR lived in a slightly more open society than they had previously experienced.[126] In some respects, East Germany was even relatively progressive, taking pride in its gender equality and social welfare programs. The DDR also provided free childcare and easier access to divorce and abortion than most Western societies.[127] The nature of ideology in East Germany meant that discrimination and class division was less prevalent than in the more tumultuous societies of Western Europe and North America. DDR citizens built unlikely fraternal bonds through such enterprises as the "Youth Pioneers" in African countries with which the SED leadership had relationships.[128]

Nevertheless, even in the more secure environment of the 1970s, the DDR regime consistently failed to provide the products its citizens desired, as evidenced by the so-

---

[125] Deutsche Welle, 'East Germany relied on forced labor', The History of East Germany, [accessed 21 October 2017], http://www.dw.com/en/east-germany-relied-on-forced-labor/a-15932840

[126] David Wilsford, *Political Leaders of Contemporary Western Europe: A Biographical Dictionary* (Westport, Connecticut: Greenwood, 1995), p. 198.

[127] Konrad H. Jarausch and Helga A. Welsh, "Two Germanies, 1961-1989", German History in Documents and Images (German Historical Institute: http://germanhistorydocs.ghi-dc.org/, [accessed 6 October 2017], p. 6.

[128] Deutsche Welle, "Africa and communist East Germany", [accessed 18 October 2017], http://www.dw.com/en/africa-and-communist-east-germany/g-18753769

called *Kaffeekrise* (Coffee Crisis) of 1977. East Germans had been enthusiastic coffee drinkers, but a rise in global prices caused a problem for the SED government. Unable to secure the hard currency necessary to pay for coffee imports, the government withdrew products from the shelves of supermarkets, effectively rationing coffee to restaurants. The resulting hardship caused an uproar amongst the population, resulting in the government developing its own variety of coffee, *Mischkaffee* (mixed coffee), consisting of 51% actual coffee mixed with additives such as chicory and sugar beet.[129] The *Kaffeekrise* passed the following year as world prices declined, but the episode demonstrated the regime's economic weakness. The culmination of this and similar privations undoubtedly played a part in undermining the regime's legitimacy in the eyes of its citizens.

Following a relatively calm period after the signing of the Basic Treaty and through *Ostpolitik* and détente, international tensions grew in the late 1970s, which helped bring to power conservative figures like Ronald Reagan in the U.S. and Margaret Thatcher in the UK. The two leaders were committed to "neoliberal" economic reform and a hard-line stance toward the communist world.

---

[129] Stefan Wolle, 'Kaffeekrise', *Die heile Welt der Diktatur. Alltag und Herrschaft in der DDR 1971-1989* (Econ&List, München 1999), [accessed 19 October 2017], http://www.ddr-wissen.de/wiki/ddr.pl?Kaffeekrise

One particular catalyst was the Soviet invasion of Afghanistan in December 1979, ostensibly to buttress the country's communist government. The incursion led to howls of protest in the West, as well as a renewed commitment to confront the Soviets and its allies. With that, East Germany and West Germany were once more to become a battleground in the latest "hot" phase of the Cold War, and Honecker could not have known that in little less than 10 years, his regime and country would lie in tatters without even a single shot fired.

Leadership was crucial in the final phase of both the Cold War and the DDR. The Soviet Union, in keeping with the communist bloc in general, churned out turgid, unimaginative, gerontocrats. Leonid Brezhnev had died in office in 1982 as Soviet general secretary, as did both of his successors, Yuri Andropov in 1984 and Konstantin Chernenko the following year. Chernenko, in particular, appeared to be frail even upon taking office. Meanwhile, Honecker was a comparatively sprightly 68 in 1980, but his mannerisms and demeanor were of a piece with his Soviet comrades.

At the same time, in the United States, Reagan came to power promising to revitalize his own country and stand up to the communist world. As a result, a new arms race began, pitting Reagan against paranoid Soviet leaders who were, no doubt, disturbed by American pronouncements that their sphere was an "Evil Empire". In this final escalation of the Cold War, Germany once more became a focal point when the Soviets deployed a new nuclear weapon–intermediate ballistic SS-20 missiles–into the territory of their Warsaw Pact allies. NATO, after much deliberation and numerous protests, responded in kind by deploying Pershing missiles into West Germany. It was Social Democrat Helmut Schmidt, nominally committed to Brandt's *Ostpolitik* but actually more hawkish toward the East, who had initially agreed to Pershing deployment. The policy was then continued with more vigor by Schmidt's successor, Helmut Kohl.

Tensions rose elsewhere in Europe also, beginning with a worker's revolt in Poland that demanded separate trade union recognition, dubbed *Solidarity*. As demonstrations continued throughout 1980-81, the Polish communist government ultimately declared martial law, partly because it feared another Soviet intervention like the one in Czechoslovakia in 1968. Though the DDR was a reliable supporter of crackdowns in the neighboring states, the unrest was just another example of the potency of the Helsinki Final Act provisions, and they were soon to surface in the DDR itself.

The SED government publicly stated its future policy direction at the 10th Party Congress in 1981, during which improving the economy, furthering foreign policy, and better relations with the BRD were all made priorities. The immediate problem for the SED government in the early 1980s, however, was mounting debt, which had increased due to global events. Two oil price shocks in the 1970s had caused inflation to soar in the West, and policy-makers eventually responded by imposing punitive interest rates, particularly when Paul Volcker became Chairman of the Federal Reserve in 1979. This, in turn, led to a world recession, making debt-repayments difficult for exposed countries and further complicating the economic difficulties of the DDR. The debt reached a peak of 11.67 billion East German Marks as the global debt crisis spiraled in 1982,[130] necessitating belt-tightening and a slight change in economic strategy. This brought about a wobbling economy, a tense international environment, and growing regional dissident activity.

This was the situation in the DDR in 1985 when the era of stagnation was almost at an end. The reform, however, came from the most unlikely of sources: the Soviet Union itself.

The End of East Germany

The USSR was in a long-period of stagnation. Its obsession with military parity with the United States had drained public finances, leading to rationing and slow

---

[130] Ferdinand Protzman, 'East Germany Losing Its Edge', *The New York Times*, 15 May 1989, [accessed 20 October 2017], http://www.nytimes.com/1989/05/15/business/east-germany-losing-its-edge.html

economic progress. In some respects, Soviet society had made great strides in terms of employment and material progress. Below the surface, however, lay dissatisfaction. Many people, aware of the stiff penalties for dissenters, presented a compliant public face while venting frustrations in private. By the early 1980s, levels of alcoholism were very high in the Soviet Union,[131] and an increasing number of casualties were being incurred in the Afghanistan conflict, their treatment upon returning home poor. It is, perhaps, unsurprising that the Politburo turned to a reformer when Chernenko died: the 54-year-old Mikhail Gorbachev.

---

[131] Sandra C. Anderson and Valerie K. Hibbs, 'Alcoholism in the Soviet Union', *International Social Work*, 35:4, (1992), pp. 441 – 453.

Gorbachev

Gorbachev was born in 1931 and rose steadily through the ranks of the Communist Party, entering the Politburo in 1980. He met arch anti-communist Margaret Thatcher in 1984, who declared, "I like Mr Gorbachev. We can do business together."[132] But neither Thatcher nor the Soviet leadership had imagined the path Gorbachev would take when he assumed power in 1985.

Most notably, he attempted to pry open the hermetically

---

[132] Margaret Thatcher, *The Downing Street Years* (London: HarperCollins, 1993), pp. 459-463.

sealed Soviet society with his signatory policies of *Glasnost* ("openness"), *Perestroika* ("restructuring"), and *Uskoreniye* ("acceleration"). Gorbachev promoted dialogue in an attempt to improve economic efficiencies and growth among other things,[133] and banned books, music, and art were suddenly allowed in this heady, yet uncertain time. Gorbachev also recognized the Soviets could not keep up with the high military spending initiated by the Reagan administration.[134] He was also very concerned about Reagan's Strategic Defense Initiative (SDI or Star Wars Project), thus subsequently taking part in a number of arms-reduction summits with the American leader.

Meanwhile, in the DDR, Honecker was alarmed by *Glasnost*. The leadership of the SED was now ossified, and dramatic liberalizing transformation was not on its agenda. Nevertheless, Gorbachev's reforms were causing change elsewhere in Europe that, along with increased contact with the West Germans, had effects within East Germany itself. The citizens of the DDR were no longer sealed off from the rest of the world, and they started to see the affluence enjoyed by their Western brethren.

The SED had permitted some relaxation of its grip by the mid-1980s, but *Glasnost* went further than Honecker and

---

[133] Godfrey Hodgson, *The People's Century: From the dawn of the century to the eve of the millennium* (Godalming: BBC Books, 1998), p. 588.
[134] Ibid, p. 589.

his allies desired. Writers, such as Mary Fulbrook, have identified the role of the church after 1978 in softening the SED's internal policies and "fostering muted dissent".[135] Therefore, even in an East Germany that was hostile to *Glasnost* and human rights, channels were being opened that eased the oppressive atmosphere on its citizens, but it also led to increasing demands for further liberalization.

Other countries in Central Europe and Eastern Europe had also begun to liberalize their economies if not their political systems, the most prominent of which was Hungary, where the regime of János Kádár allowed some moderate market-based reforms. Hungary had suffered many of the same problems as the DDR, such as a crisis in hard currency and material progress, though on the face of things, East Germany seemed to be in a stronger position than Hungary. Nevertheless, the cracks in the solidarity and homogeneity of the "Eastern bloc" would undermine the SED in East Germany. Gorbachev apparently took a more relaxed approach to Soviet control of its Central European and East European satellites, which became formalized at the end of 1988 when he gave a speech to the United Nations General Assembly on December 7 that would have genuinely revolutionary implications. As well as endorsing the Helsinki process and human rights, the Soviet leader announced he was withdrawing all his

[135] Mary Fulbrook, *History of Germany, 1918-2000: the divided nation* (Oxford: Blackwell, 2002), p. 59.

forces from Afghanistan. He then turned to Central Europe and Eastern Europe and said, "By agreement with our Warsaw Treaty allies, we have decided to withdraw by 1991 six tank divisions from East Germany, Czechoslovakia and Hungary, and to disband them. Assault landing troops and several other formations and units, including assault crossing units with their weapons and combat equipment, will also be withdrawn from the groups of Soviet forces stationed in those countries."[136]

This essentially marked the end of the "Brezhnev Doctrine" that had been in existence since the invasion of Czechoslovakia in 1968. In effect, Gorbachev had granted these countries autonomy from the USSR, which was later reinforced by another Soviet official in 1989, who had declared the "Sinatra Doctrine." Pursuant to this, the Central European and Eastern European states could, to quote the American crooner Frank Sinatra, "go their own way".[137] This effectively ended Soviet communism's iron hold over Poland, Hungary, Czechoslovakia, Romania, and East Germany, and it also opened these nations' regimes up to challenge from opposition groups.

At that stage, it was unclear as to how they might respond, but the first communist state to significantly

---

[136] The Gorbachev Visit; Excerpts From Speech to U.N. on Major Soviet Military Cuts, 8 December 1988, [accessed 26 October 2017], http://www.nytimes.com/1988/12/08/world/the-gorbachev-visit-excerpts-from-speech-to-un-on-major-soviet-military-cuts.html?pagewanted=all

[137] Mary Fulbrook, *History of Germany, 1918-2000: the divided nation* (Oxford: Blackwell, 2002), p. 261.

challenge the new situation was Poland in 1989. The government of General Wojciech Jaruzelski called "Round Table" talks with solidarity leaders, including the charismatic Lech Walesa. To the surprise of many outsiders, the outcome of the talks led to semi-free elections and a transition to a non-communist government. Hungary then relaxed its border with Austria as part of its own reforms. Around 220,000 East Germans went on holiday in Hungary in the summer of 1989,[138] facilitating some 900 citizens to make a dash for freedom in the West after seeing the unprotected barrier.[139] In the end, their attempts were unimpeded.

This single move by the Hungarian government would be another catalyst hastening the demise of East Germany, as the trickle soon became a flood, reigniting the issue the SED had attempted to quash 28 years previously with the construction of the Berlin Wall. The Hungarian government's border relaxation led to a new surge of migration from East Germany to West Germany as 13,000 East Germans traveled from their state through Czechoslovakia and then Hungary, across the recently opened "Iron Curtain" into Austria, and then onto West Germany. For the Bonn government and the West in general, this was a huge propaganda victory, and the West

---

[138] Ibid.

[139] W. Mayr, 'Hungary's Peaceful Revolution Cutting the Fence and Changing History', *Der Spiegel*, 29 May 2009, http://www.spiegel.de/international/europe/hungary-s-peaceful-revolution-cutting-the-fence-and-changing-history-a-627632.html, [accessed 31 October 2017]

Germans welcomed the refugees as heroes, packing train stations to see them arrive.[140] The West German government even gave the newcomers *Begrüßungsgeld* ("welcome money") of up to 100 Deutsche Marks.

Enthusiasm in the West soon began to wane as the numbers increased[141], but for the SED government in Berlin, Hungary's move and the resulting exodus was both embarrassing and frustrating. Honecker's regime was, in fact, furious, aware that migration and the pressure of *Glasnost* was rapidly becoming an existential threat to the state's legitimacy. The Hungarian government responded to SED complaints by stating it was simply complying with international refugee commitments, which, of course, had been ignored prior to Gorbachev's "Sinatra Doctrine".[142]

East German migrants also attempted to claim refuge at the West German embassy in Prague. At its peak, 8,000 people crammed onto the grounds of the embassy, causing leading West German politicians, such as Foreign Minister Hans-Dietrich Genscher, to visit the embassy to try to broker a way around the impasse. In the end, the SED government permitted "sealed trains" to take

---

[140] Mary Fulbrook, *History of Germany, 1918-2000: the divided nation* (Oxford: Blackwell, 2002), pp. 261-262.

[141] Christiane Gläser, '100 DM Begrüßungsgeld Auf den Mauerfall folgte der Einkaufsrausch', *Berliner Zeitung*, [accessed 31 October 2017], https://www.berliner-zeitung.de/461498, Mary Fulbrook, *History of Germany, 1918-2000: the divided nation* (Oxford: Blackwell, 2002), p. 262.

[142] Mary Fulbrook, *History of Germany, 1918-2000: the divided nation* (Oxford: Blackwell, 2002), p. 261.

refugees to West Germany, covering the crisis up by labeling them "irresponsible antisocial traitors and criminals".[143]

As was the case in the 1950s and early 1960s, the sight of desperate citizens fleeing their country inevitably cast the East German state in a very poor light, and unlike the earlier years, the exodus quickly spread to demonstrations within the DDR itself. A number of civil society groups formed to demand political reform in the autumn of 1989, the most notable of which were the protests in Leipzig. After the regular Monday evening church service in the *Nikolaikirche* ("Nicholas Church"), peaceful protesters formed a procession through the city calling for democratization. Similar demonstrations occurred in East Berlin and the cities of Halle, Plauen, and Dresden.[144]

Honecker's regime appeared to be preparing for a crackdown. On October 3, 1989, visa-free travel to Czechoslovakia was banned, effectively quarantining the entire population.[145] Honecker was more interested in putting on a brave face for the 40th-anniversary

[143] Norman M. Naimark, *The Russians in Germany: A History of the Soviet Zone of Occupation, 1945-1949* (Harvard: Harvard University Press, 1995), pp. 132, 133, Ferdinand Protzman, 'Jubilant East Germans Cross to West in Sealed Trains', *New York Times*, 6 October 1989, http://www.nytimes.com/1989/10/06/world/jubilant-east-germans-cross-to-west-in-sealed-trains.html, [accessed 28 October 2017]

[144] Peter Wensierski, 'Die WG der Rebellen', *Der Spiegel*, 3 October 2014, http://www.spiegel.de/einestages/leipzig-wie-es-1989-zur-montagsdemonstration-kam-a-993513.html, [accessed 31 October 2017], Mary Fulbrook, *History of Germany, 1918-2000: the divided nation* (Oxford: Blackwell, 2002), p. 264.

[145] Mary Fulbrook, *History of Germany, 1918-2000: the divided nation* (Oxford: Blackwell, 2002), p. 265.

celebration of the state, on October 7, and the festivities went ahead as planned, but the atmosphere was, by all accounts, strangely subdued.[146] Gorbachev was in attendance and sensed the pressure bubbling beneath the surface, urging Honecker to embrace reform and telling the ailing dictator that "he who is too late is punished by life."[147]

Two days later, a further protest was planned in Leipzig[148] only this time the army, police, and Stasi were on the streets and hospitals were reportedly stocked full of blood, ready for transfusions in the event of violence. There were concerns the SED would adopt a "Chinese Solution" to the protests, following the brutal crackdown on pro-democracy demonstrations in Tiananmen Square in May that year.[149]

To the surprise of many, the protests peacefully passed as security forces effectively stood down, but events then gathered pace. Honecker was forced to step down at a Politburo meeting on October 18, and many other of the top officials soon followed. The visa-free travel ban to

[146] *Der Spiegel*, 'How 'Gorbi' Spoiled East Germany's 40th Birthday Party', 7 October 1989, http://www.spiegel.de/international/germany/oct-7-1989-how-gorbi-spoiled-east-germany-s-40th-birthday-party-a-653724.html, [accessed 31 October 2017]

[147] Godfrey Hodgson, *The People's Century: From the dawn of the century to the eve of the millennium* (Godalming: BBC Books, 1998), p. 592.

[148] Andrew Curry, ''We Are the People' A Peaceful Revolution in Leipzig', *Der Spiegel*, 9 October 2009, http://www.spiegel.de/international/germany/we-are-the-people-a-peaceful-revolution-in-leipzig-a-654137.html, [accessed 1 November 2017]

[149] Robert Hutchings, 'American Diplomacy and the End of the Cold War in Europe', *Foreign Policy Breakthroughs: Cases in Successful Diplomacy*, ed. Robert Hutchings and Jeremi Suri (Oxford: Oxford University Press, 2015, pp. 148-172), p. 150.

Czechoslovakia was lifted on October 27, and more "liberal" communists, such as Hans Modrow, entered the Politburo while Egon Krenz became general secretary.[150] Demonstrations continued in the major cities, and between 500,000 and 1 million took to the streets of Berlin on November 4.[151]

In the months that led to the fall of the Berlin Wall, pubic protest grew almost daily, and after so many years of repression by Stasi agents, many Germans participating were surprised at the fact that demonstrations were allowed to move forward. Though many demonstrators were subject to beatings and arrest, the crowds gathering in Eastern churches grew each week. "Demonstrators in Leipzig and other cities proclaimed popular sovereignty with the slogan 'Wir sind das Volk', or 'We are the People'", reported John Leslie, a student interning with the NBC nightly news program in Leipzig and other eastern cities. This phrase would later morph to "We are one people" as Easterners grew bolder to challenge the Socialist government's claims to being the People's Republic and the crowds desired to identify themselves more boldly.[152]

---

[150] Mary Fulbrook, *History of Germany, 1918-2000: the divided nation* (Oxford: Blackwell, 2002), p. 267.

[151] Ibid.

[152] John Leslie, "The Fall of the Berlin Wall Twenty Years Later: John Leslie Provides Remembrances of 1989 from Inside East Germany," New Zealand International Review 34, no. 5 (2009), https://www.questia.com/read/1G1-207943787.

Only a few months before the fall of the Wall, John Leslie was invited to be a part of a discussion between East German officials and their West German guests. At the event, one of the party secretaries was asked for his thoughts on the repercussions of East German youth being able to witness the stirring revolutions in Poland, Hungary, and the Soviet Union on television. The secretary replied first to the East German student who was translating for the English speaking students: "Too many of our citizens spend too much time watching television and not enough time building socialism!" At this point the Cambridge-educated East German translator remarked that she saw the response as "ideological, heavy-handed and defensive". This is another illustration of the disconnect that existed between East German youth and those in East Germany who were old enough to have been convinced that the harsh repression and lack of freedom were at worst inevitable and at best protection against the Western fascists who could otherwise overtake them.[153]

Though the peaceful demonstrations in Berlin were not ended in a Tiananmen-style crackdown, the Stasi made sure that the protestors felt their presence. Stasi police were stationed outside of the churches to intercept those protestors who exited. Those deemed "guilty" of incitement, speaking against the state, or other "crimes"

---

[153] Ibid.

were taken to be interrogated, had their names and pictures recorded, and were humiliated in various states of undress as the Stasi force them to sign statements incriminating themselves.[154]

In the years following the fall of the Berlin Wall, many writers have taken the time to analyze the event chronologically. Just how did the messages about the easing of travel restrictions get to the people? What was the East German government's intention versus how was it implemented by the people who carried it out? Before attempting an answer to these questions, it is important to note that the fall of the Berlin Wall was in no way inevitable, at least in the sense of when and how it took place. Timothy Garten Ash cautions his *Guardian* readers regarding the tendency to view it this way, writing that "it is almost impossible to recreate the emotional intensity of the moment of liberation. For that intensity came from having lived for most, if not all, your life with the aching certainty that something like this was, precisely, impossible".[155]

In another warning to readers who assume the fall of the wall was simply a foregone conclusion, historian David Clay Large reminds his readers that East Germany and its leaders had perhaps the least reason to believe they were

---

[154] Borneman 23.

[155] Timothy Garten Ash. "The Fall of the Berlin Wall: What it Meant to Be There." The Guardian. 6 November 2014. Web.

in danger. Honecker, Large claims, had a great amount of credibility as the head of Germany since the end of World War II, and had done a very effective job at squelching dissidence. As had been the practice of East Germany since the construction of the Berlin Wall and the accompanying economic struggles, dissidents could become prisoners, who would then become saleable goods to West Germany.[156] The severity of response to those who desired escape and the internal intimidation of East Germans in their workplaces, homes, and even churches gave many Germans reason enough to believe that they would live and die in the shadow of the wall. After 28 years, there were now many living who had never known a day without it.

In the end, however, the pressure mounted on even East Germany to make concessions. Though Honecker disagreed with Gorbachev's reform attempts, it was still difficult when "GDR authorities found themselves in the awkward position of trying to curtail contacts between East German citizens and the mother country of communism".[157] The people of East Germany had limited chances for public gatherings without strict control. In January of 1988, East German leaders had gathered to honor the communist radical Rosa Luxemburg. When a number of protestors displayed a banner with a quote from

---

[156] Large 520.
[157] Ibid.

the communist heroine ("True Freedom is Always the Freedom of the Non-conformists"), they were immediately arrested and exiled from the country.[158]

Finally, tensions between East Germany and her resentful neighbors had reached a breaking point. With literally tens of thousands of East German refugees clogging the streets, highways, and embassies of her neighbor nations, it was up to East Germany to ease travel restrictions and make some concessions to stem the tide, so the decision was made to allow travel outside of East Berlin for one month to those with proper passports. Large notes that the number of East Germans with proper passports was so low that this would not have caused a high influx of travel outside of the borders. However, the hastily called press conference and the rewriting of the policy up to the last hour meant that a mistake would be made that would change the world as the Germans knew it.

Guenter Schabowski was the official spokesperson at a press conference that was being televised live throughout East Germany. Charged with delivering the new travel guidelines in a hastily-called press conference, Schabowski began his remarks: "You see, comrades, I was informed today…that such an announcement had been…distributed earlier today. You should actually have

---

[158] Large, 520.

it already…1) 'Applications for travel abroad by private individuals can now be made without the previously existing requirements (of demonstrating a need to travel or proving familial relationships). The travel authorizations will be issued within a short time. Grounds for denial will only be applied in particular exceptional cases. The responsible departments of passport and registration control in the People's Police district offices in the GDR are instructed to issue visas for permanent exit without delays and without presentation of the existing requirements for permanent exit.'"

After being asked when it would come into effect, Schabowski replied, "That comes into effect, according to my information, immediately, without delay." When asked if it also applies for West Berlin, he responded, "Permanent exit can take place via all border crossings from the GDR to the FRG and West Berlin, respectively."[159]

[159] Guenter Schabowski, "Guenter Schabowski's Press Conference in the GDR International Press Center," Making the History of 1989, Item #449, http://chnm.gmu.edu/1989/items/show/449 (accessed February 27 2015, 8:28 pm).

Picture of the press conference

The Wall Street Journal speculated that Schabowski had faltered not because he had not prepared carefully enough, as some charged, but because he was "not used to scrutiny by a free press…[And] he couldn't deal with rapid-fire questions from international journalists".[160] Whatever the real cause of Schabowski's struggle to communicate, it became immediately clear that "seeming accidents have the power to shape history".[161] Later, American journalist Tom Brokaw would recall following Schakowsky upstairs after the conference had concluded and asking him to re-

---

[160] Walker, Marcus. "Did Journalists' Questions Topple the Berlin Wall?" The Wall Street Journal. 7 November 2014.
[161] Stern 459.

read the portion of the brief that lifted the travel restrictions on border crossings between East and West Berlin directly. It was then, Brokaw realized, that the end of the Berlin Wall had come. In his newscast, he told the watching world, "This is a historic night…. The East German Government has just declared that East German citizens will be able to cross the wall … without restrictions."[162] Schabowski would be expelled from the party but fail to escape prosecution as a high Politburo official; he served only a few months of a three-year sentence after distancing himself from communist ideals.

On the evening of November 9th, 1989, Harald Jaeger, an East German border guard, watched a television as he ate a meal at the canteen before arriving for his guard duty shift at the Berlin Wall that night at 6:00 p.m. Hearing the removal of travel restrictions would take place "immediately", he remembers "almost choking on my bread roll". He arrived at the wall to find other skeptical guards and made multiple telephone calls to his superiors, attempting to get clarification about what to do with the now gathering crowds. At first, Jaeger's superiors simply ignored his question, telling them to send people without authorization home. After realizing the seriousness of the situation, however, Jaeger was instructed to let the "most

---

[162] Melvyn P. Leffler, "Chapter 5: Dreams of Freedom, Temptations of Power," in The Fall of the Berlin Wall: The Revolutionary Legacy of 1989, ed. Jeffrey A. Engel (New York: Oxford University Press, 2009), 136,

agitated" members of the crowd pass through to West Berlin in hopes of appeasing them. Obviously, the opposite effect was achieved and Jaeger had no further instruction from his superiors. Fearing for the safety of the burgeoning crowd, Jaeger delivered the order to open the border between East and West Berlin at 11:30 p.m.[163] Thus, Jaeger is most often credited with being the man who actually "took down" the Wall.

Another East German border guard, Erich Wittman, recalled his memory of the evening: "I was promoted to Corporal, and was directly posted as the Officer of the main checkpoint of the Berlin wall. I still remember the tensions, thousands of cars was in front of me, honking and wanted me to move, which I refused….The news of the Berlin wall being open for anyone hadn't reached us who were posted at the wall, only when my girlfriend, who I for the first time on [sic] months seen, came to me and told me about it. I was in shock and didn't know what to do, all around me, thousands of people started to gather around me, climbing over the wall, some even brought tools and sledge-hammers and started to destroy the wall, the people kept yelling at us as we told them to stay back, then…On the TV, which I saw through the window of the Guard's Resting place, I could see the politicians ordering the opening to West Berlin for everyone, I ordered the

[163] "Former border guard Harald Jaeger recalls how he opened the Berlin Wall." South China Morning Post. 6 November 2014.

soldiers to open the gates and let the cars pass, the yells formed into cheers and all over us, people came to hug me and my men, and the cars kept swarming over the border. Erika grabbed onto my uniform, and pulled me to her, and hugged me, I responded in kissing her, then a camera man appeared on the scene and filmed the opening of the wall, and got us on tape…The supreme officer came to me later, asked me why the people are flooding over to West Germany, I told him. The German Democratic Republic is dead, they announced it on Television, open your borders as well for these people. He quickly went away, and all over East Germany the news came, and the Berlin wall was flooded by people over several days."

A crane removing pieces of the wall in December 1989

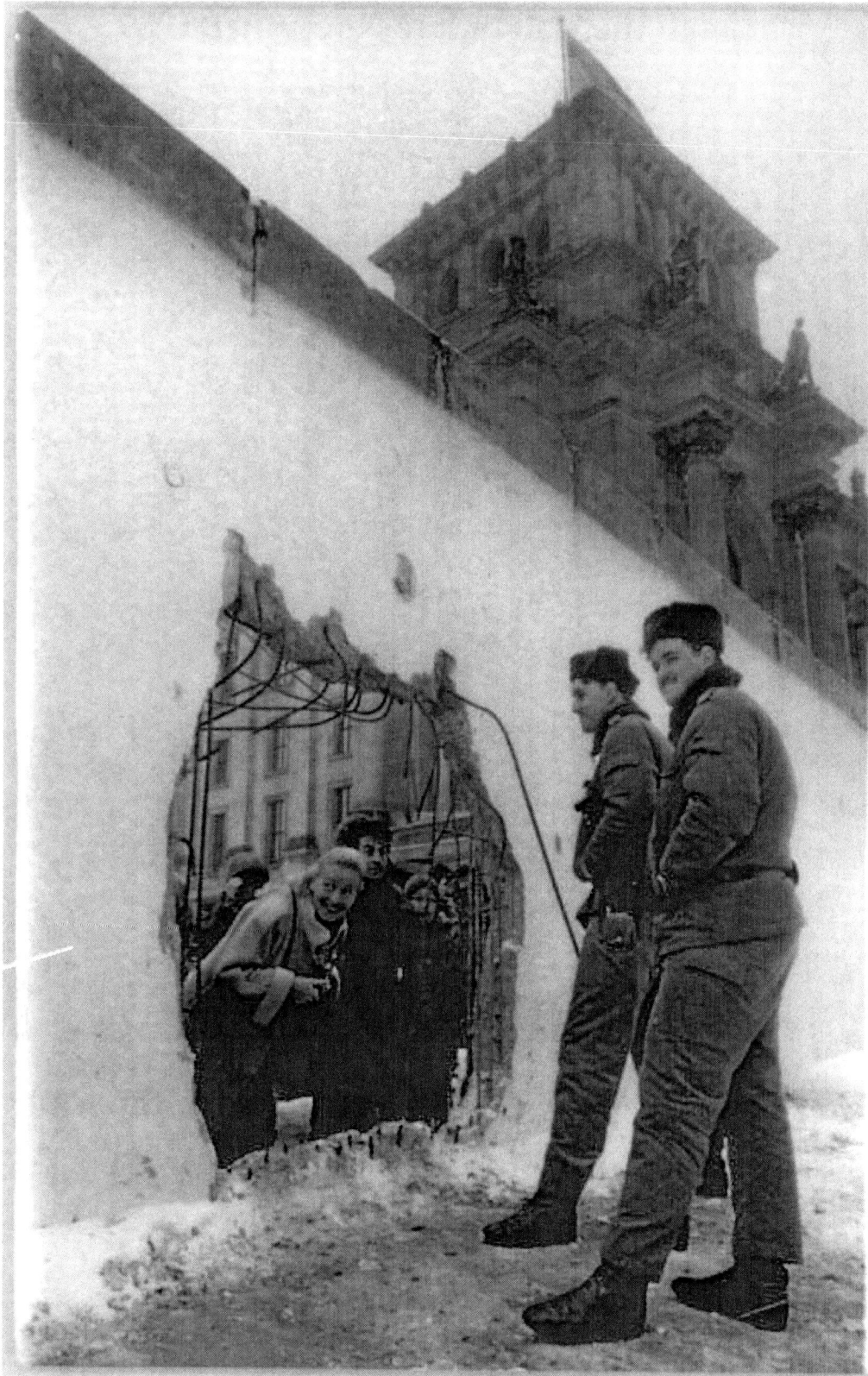

Pictures of East Germans talking to West Germans

**1990 picture of the graffiti and pieces of the wall
chipped away**

The Race to Reunification

The world had been taken by surprise when the Berlin
Wall came down, and Helmut Kohl wasted no time in
asserting himself regarding the situation. On November

28, Kohl gave a speech setting out "Ten Points" that would lead to greater German cooperation, and eventually even reunification.[164] The concessions made in the 1972 Basic Treaty had apparently been forgotten, and the pre-1972 policy of incorporating the whole of Germany within one democratic state was back on the table.

Though Kohl's objectives appeared ambitious, it was thought the Soviets would not accept a unified Germany as part of NATO, and two of West Germany's closest allies, Britain and France, were opposed to unification, fearing Germany might try to dominate Europe as it had attempted to do in the first half of the 20th century. Margaret Thatcher, in an interview outside 10 Downing Street, warned that talk of German reunification was much, much "too fast" and that East Germany would be required to show its development as a democracy before that could be taken under serious consideration. Despite issuing cautions about the pace at which reunification should take place and the idea that it was impossible for all East Germans to leave the country[165], Thatcher did take a moment to delight in the historical moment: "I think it is a great day for freedom. I watched the scenes on

[164] The German Chancellery, 'The Federal Chancellor, Helmut Kohl; 1982-1998', [accessed 31 October 2017], https://www.bundeskanzlerin.de/Webs/BKin/EN/Chancellery/Timeline_Federal_Chancellors_since_1949/Kohl/kohl_node.html, Robert Hutchings, 'American Diplomacy and the End of the Cold War in Europe', *Foreign Policy Breakthroughs: Cases in Successful Diplomacy*, ed. Robert Hutchings and Jeremi Suri (Oxford: Oxford University Press, 2015, pp. 148-172), p. 160.

[165] Thatcher, Margaret. "Remarks on the Berlin Wall (fall thereof)". Thatcher Archive: COI transcript. 10 November 1989.

television last night and again this morning because I felt one ought not only hear about them but see them because you see the joy on people's faces and you see what freedom means to them; it makes you realize that you cannot stifle or suppress people's desire for liberty and so I watched with the same joy as everyone else."[166]

Kohl had one crucial ally on the matter, however, and that was President George H.W. Bush.[167] High-level diplomacy accelerated throughout 1990. The SED had appointed Hans Modrow as Prime Minister, and he made the fateful decision to relinquish one-party rule. In March of that year, East Germany held its first elections since 1946, and in this election, many of the same parties stood in East Germany that had existed in West Germany, such as Kohl's Christian Democratic Union (CDU), the center-left Social Democrats (SPD), and the renamed SED (as the Party of Democratic Socialism (PDS)). The CDU won the election with 41% of the vote and formed a "grand" coalition with the SPD. Crucially, the CDU stood on a program supporting reunification with the West, so the first truly democratically elected government in the DDR's history was short-lived. The caretaker leader, Lothar de Maizière, appointed a novice politician as his spokesperson, a 35-year-old woman named Angela

[166] Ibid.
[167] John Campbell, *Margaret Thatcher Volume Two: The Iron Lady* (London: Random House, 2004), p. 629

Merkel. On September 20, 1990, the DDR's *Volkskammer* voted for a reunification treaty, effectively dissolving their own parliament and state.[168]

The two Germanys were hopelessly uneven economically. In an attempt to align the two systems, the governments in Bonn and Berlin decided to replace the East German Mark with the West German *Deutsche Mark*. Surprisingly, given the much greater strength of the West German currency, conversion of East German Marks was granted at a 1:1 parity, thus starting the huge subsidization of the former East Germany by the former West Germany. West German legal norms and rules were also introduced during 1990.

Ultimately, Kohl was able to gain agreement from the major powers over German unification, and the new Germany was accepted into NATO and the European Community (later the EU). Britain's Thatcher lost the argument and had to relent when President Mitterrand of France dropped his opposition. The talks essentially secured German acquiescence to the French plan for a more integrated European Union, including a proposed single currency, requiring, of course, German funding. President Bush was strongly in favor of German reunification and Gorbachev, whose own power was

---

[168] "Politics in Germany: The Online Edition", University of California, Irvine, [accessed 30 October 2017], http://www.socsci.uci.edu/~rdalton/germany/ch2/chap2.htm

rapidly fading, also agreed. Due to Kohl's energetic diplomacy and the enthusiastic acceptance by East Germans themselves, Germany was reunified on October 3, 1990, less than a year after the fall of the Berlin Wall, and the country's first elections were held that December.

In 1990 and 1991, Gorbachev tried to preserve the Soviet Union in a less centralized form that would grant some form of home rule to the Soviet republics. However, in 1991, Soviet hardliners began to organize a coup against Gorbachev, who they saw as responsible for the rapid deterioration of the Soviet Union and its communist allies in Eastern Europe. The coup plotters executed their plan in August 1991, attempting to confine Gorbachev to his summer residence and restore the supremacy of the Communist Party. Boris Yeltsin, one of Gorbachev's top aides, organized popular resistance to the coup and ultimately defeated it.

In the months after the coup, 10 former Soviet republics declared their independence. Russia, long the dominant member of the Soviet Union, followed on December 12, 1991. Within two weeks, the Soviet Union would be officially dissolved.

East Germany's Legacy

East Germany was initially considered an unloved state and welcome casualty of the upheaval of the late 1980s and early 1990s, which is no surprise given that it was oppressive and almost literally imprisoned its citizens while restraining them both materially and politically. The revelations that emerged about the Stasi shocked the world in the early 1990s when they were suspected of burning files, resulting in demands from East German citizens for transparency and justice. The German government declassified Stasi records in 1992, revealing surveillance material that, at its height, included records on 6 million people, a full third of the entire population. The scope of this internal spying, coercion, and harassment left a long shadow over German society.

The cost of absorbing East Germany into a reunified Federal Republic has been high. West German taxpayers have had to pay a 5% levy in order to develop and rehabilitate the East Germans, a levy that continues to this day. Indeed, reunification took such a heavy toll on Germany that by the late 1990s, it had been dubbed the "sick man of Europe" due to its economic weakness.[169] This makes it all the more remarkable that by the time of the Euro crisis, beginning in 2009, Germany – now led by former East German citizen Angela Merkel - had, by far, the biggest economy and political clout in Europe.

The years since the demise of East Germany have led

---

[169] *The Economist*, 'The sick man of the euro', 3 June 1999, [accessed 30 October 2017], http://www.economist.com/node/209559

many in the region to reappraise the state. East Germans have not fully adapted to the harsh economic realities of market capitalism, and some have described their unhappiness at being treated by Westerners as second-class citizens, which the derogatory term "Ossis" (Easterners) encapsulates. Nostalgia for East Germany, or *Ostalgie*, has increased since the turn of the century, and a more insidious pattern of anti-immigrant sentiment has emerged in a land once known for fraternal links and Youth Pioneers with other countries around the world. This was clear almost as soon as the new Germany had formed, from its anti-immigrant riots in Rostock in 1992 until the present, and the popularity of the anti-immigrant Alternative Für Deutschland (AfD) in the 2017 parliamentary elections.

East Germany existed for little over 40 years, a socialist experiment closely linked with the geopolitics of the Cold War. The legacy of the state, however, is certainly still around, and it looks likely to continue for the foreseeable future.

Online Resources

Other German history titles by Charles River Editors

Other titles about East Germany on Amazon

Further Reading

Sandra C. Anderson and Valerie K. Hibbs, 'Alcoholism in the Soviet Union', *International Social Work*, 35:4, (1992)

Gary Bruce, *Resistance with the people: repression and resistance in Eastern Germany, 1945 – 1955* (Oxford: Rowman & Littlefield, 2003)

University of California, "Politics in Germany: The Online Edition", University of California, Irvine, [accessed 30 October 2017], http://www.socsci.uci.edu/~rdalton/germany/ch2/chap2.htm

John Campbell, *Margaret Thatcher Volume Two: The Iron Lady* (London: Random House, 2004)

Andrew Curry, ''We Are the People' A Peaceful Revolution in Leipzig', *Der Spiegel*, 9 October 2009, http://www.spiegel.de/international/germany/we-are-the-people-a-peaceful-revolution-in-leipzig-a-654137.html, [accessed 1 November 2017]

Der Spiegel, 'How 'Gorbi' Spoiled East Germany's 40th Birthday Party', 7 October 1989, http://www.spiegel.de/international/germany/oct-7-1989-how-gorbi-spoiled-east-germany-s-40th-birthday-party-a-653724.html, [accessed 31 October 2017]

Deutsche Welle, "Africa and communist East Germany", [accessed 18 October 2017], http://www.dw.com/en/africa-and-communist-east-germany/g-18753769

Deutsche Welle, 'East Germany relied on forced labor', The History of East Germany, [accessed 21 October 2017], http://www.dw.com/en/east-germany-relied-on-forced-labor/a-15932840

The Economist, 'The sick man of the euro', 3 June 1999, [accessed 30 October 2017], http://www.economist.com/node/209559

Andrew Evans, "The Last Gasp of Socialism: Economics and Culture in 1960s East Germany", *German Life and Letters*, (63, 2010, pp. 331–344)

Christiane Gläser, '100 DM Begrüßungsgeld Auf den Mauerfall folgte der Einkaufsrausch', *Berliner Zeitung*, [accessed 31 October 2017], https://www.berliner-zeitung.de/461498

Anna von der Goltz, "Attraction and Aversion in Germany's '1968': Encountering the Western Revolt in East Berlin", *Journal of Contemporary History*, (50:3, 2014, pp. 536 – 559)

Godfrey Hodgson, *The People's Century: From the dawn of the century to the eve of the millennium*

(Godalming: BBC Books, 1998)

Niall Ferguson, *Kissinger 1923-1968: The Idealist* (London: Allen Lane, 2015)

Mary Fulbrook, *History of Germany, 1918-2000: the divided nation* (Oxford: Blackwell, 2002)

The German Chancellery, 'The Federal Chancellor, Helmut Kohl; 1982-1998', [accessed 31 October 2017], https://www.bundeskanzlerin.de/Webs/BKin/EN/Chancellery/Timeline_Federal_Chancellors_since_1949/Kohl/kohl_node.html

William Glenn Gray, *Germany's Cold War: The Global Campaign to Isolate East Germany, 1949-1969* (London: University of North Carolina Press, 2003)

Robert Hutchings, 'American Diplomacy and the End of the Cold War in Europe', *Foreign Policy Breakthroughs: Cases in Successful Diplomacy*, ed. Robert Hutchings and Jeremi Suri (Oxford: Oxford University Press, 2015, pp. 148-172)

Konrad H. Jarausch and Helga A. Welsh, "Two Germanies, 1961-1989", German History in Documents and Images (German Historical Institute: http://germanhistorydocs.ghi-dc.org/, [accessed 6 October 2017]

Gerald Knaus, 'Europe and Azerbaijan: The End of Shame', *Journal of Democracy*, (26:3, July 2015, pp. 5-18)

Giles MacDonogh, *After the Reich : from the fall of Vienna to the Berlin airlift* (London: John Murray, 2007)

W. Mayr, 'Hungary's Peaceful Revolution Cutting the Fence and Changing History', *Der Spiegel*, 29 May 2009, http://www.spiegel.de/international/europe/hungary-s-peaceful-revolution-cutting-the-fence-and-changing-history-a-627632.html, [accessed 31 October 2017]

Norman M. Naimark, *The Russians in Germany: A History of the Soviet Zone of Occupation, 1945-1949* (Harvard: Harvard University Press, 1995)

The Gorbachev Visit; Excerpts From Speech to U.N. on Major Sovict Military Cuts, *New York Times*, 8 December 1988, [accessed 26 October 2017], http://www.nytimes.com/1988/12/08/world/the-gorbachev-visit-excerpts-from-speech-to-un-on-major-soviet-military-cuts.html?pagewanted=all

Christian Ostermann, *Uprising in East Germany, 1953 : the Cold War, the German question, and the first major upheaval behind the Iron Curtain* (Budapest: Central

European Press, 2001)

Thomas Parrish, *Berlin in the balance, 1945 - 1949 : the blockade, the airlift, the first mayor battle of the Cold War* (Reading: Addison Wesley, 1998)

Ferdinand Protzman, 'East Germany Losing Its Edge', *New York Times*, 15 May 1989, [accessed 20 October 2017], http://www.nytimes.com/1989/05/15/business/east-germany-losing-its-edge.html

Ferdinand Protzman, 'Jubilant East Germans Cross to West in Sealed Trains', *New York Times*, 6 October 1989, http://www.nytimes.com/1989/10/06/world/jubilant-east-germans-cross-to-west-in-sealed-trains.html, [accessed 28 October 2017]

Albrecht Ritschl and Tamás Vonyó, "The roots of economic failure: what explains East Germany's falling behind between 1945 and 1950?", *European Review of Economic History*, (18:2, 1 May 2014, pp. 166–184)

Paul H Robinson, Sarah M. Robinson, *Pirates, Prisoners, and Lepers: Lessons from Life Outside the Law*, (University of Nebraska Press, 2015)

M.E. Sarotte, *Dealing with the Devil : East Germany, Detente, and Ostpolitik, 1969-1973,* (The University of

North Carolina Press, 2001)

Edith Sheffer, "On Edge: Building the Border in East and West Germany," *Central European History*, (40:2, 2007, pp. 307–339)

Margaret Thatcher, *The Downing Street Years* (London: HarperCollins, 1993)

Henry Thomson, "Repression, Redistribution and the Problem of Authoritarian Control*", East European Politics and Societies*, (31: 1, 2017, pp. 68 – 92)

Peter Wensierski, 'Die WG der Rebellen', *Der Spiegel*, 3 October 2014, http://www.spiegel.de/einestages/leipzig-wie-es-1989-zur-montagsdemonstration-kam-a-993513.html, [accessed 31 October 2017]

David Wilsford, *Political Leaders of Contemporary Western Europe: A Biographical Dictionary* (Westport, Connecticut: Greenwood, 1995)

Gareth M. Winrow, *The Foreign Policy of the GDR in Africa* (Cambridge: Cambridge University Press, 1990)

Gregory R. Witkowski, "Peasants Revolt? Re-evaluating the 17 June Uprising in East Germany", *German History*, (24:2, 1 April 2006, pp. 243–266)

Stefan Wolle, 'Kaffeekrise', *Die heile Welt der Diktatur. Alltag und Herrschaft in der DDR 1971-1989*

(Econ&List, München 1999), [accessed 19 October 2017], http://www.ddr-wissen.de/wiki/ddr.pl?Kaffeekrise

Free Books by Charles River Editors

We have brand new titles available for free most days of the week. To see which of our titles are currently free, click on this link.

Discounted Books by Charles River Editors

We have titles at a discount price of just 99 cents everyday. To see which of our titles are currently 99 cents, click on this link.

CPSIA information can be obtained
at www.ICGtesting.com
Printed in the USA
LVOW09s1736120218
566273LV00004B/31/P

9 781981 245987